My first day as a volunteer at Fort Indiantown Gap was a heartbreaking one. I handed out sandwiches, soup, and lemonade to Vietnamese strangers who did not know how to talk my language and were still too shocked to smile.

I didn't sleep well that night. . . . I was restless. The next day I was riding the tractor . . . mowing the lawn and enjoying the beautiful surroundings of our spacious Owl Valley home.

My mind wandered back to our daughter's gorgeous garden reception . . . held amidst delicate yellow flowers in contrast with velvet green grass. I remembered her as she stood . . . a radiant, beautiful bride beneath the white trellis.

But slowly my daughter's lovely face seemed to fade and her precious image was replaced by those nameless, quiet strangers I had seen at the Gap the day before. I had a vision of an oriental girl standing on the lawn!

Suddenly . . . above the sound of the tractor . . . I heard the Lord say clearly and distinctly, "I'm ready now. Are you?"

He was accepting the commitment I had made to Him fourteen months earlier. He was ready to use our house!

# Take This House

Evamae Barton Crist

Introduction by
Frances Hunter

HERALD PRESS
Scottdale, Pennsylvania
Kitchener, Ontario

TAKE THIS HOUSE



Published simultaneously in Canada by Herald Press, Kitchener, Ont. N2G 4M5
International Standard Book Number: 0-8361-1817-0
Printed in the United States of America
Design: Alice B. Shetler

10 9 8 7 6 5 4 3

He protects the immigrants.

Psalm 146:9, *The Living Bible*.

Dedicated to
JESUS CHRIST
who has blessed me abundantly
above all that I ask or think . . .
far more than I deserve

# Contents

# Introduction

*Total commitment!* Two words that express so much in such little space. I often wonder if any of us ever realize what God will ask of us when we are willing to step over that line between partial and total commitment!

In my own life I never realized what God would require of me, and it's just as well, because if I had known, I might never have made the commitment.

Evamae Crist felt the Spirit of God tugging on her heartstrings without realizing what the consequences would be. I'm sure she would have backed out had she known in advance.

God is so good, because He keeps us from making the mistake of withdrawing before we receive the blessing. Evamae's unique story held me from the very first sentence to the last note of victory, and it will do the same for you.

May it challenge you to throw your life recklessly away for the cause of Jesus Christ!

*Frances Hunter*
Houston, Texas

Director . . . . . . . . . . . . . GOD
Producer . . . . . . . . . . . . JESUS CHRIST
Prompter . . . . . . . . . . . . HIS HOLY SPIRIT

## CAST OF CHARACTERS
(not necessarily in order of appearance)

EVAMAE . . . . . . . . . . . assertive and caring
DALE . . . . . . . . . . . . . . strong and thoughtful
DONG. . . . . . . . . . . . . . fatherly and determined
ANH . . . . . . . . . . . . . . . loving and gracious
QUYEN . . . . . . . . . . . . studious and reserved
VIET . . . . . . . . . . . . . . . playful and enthusiastic
NGUYEN . . . . . . . . . . . quiet and intelligent
PHUONG . . . . . . . . . . . funny and warm
BABY JOHN . . . . . . . . cuddly and observant
VU . . . . . . . . . . . . . . . . . friendly and willing
GRANDMOTHER LE matriarchal and gentle

The above list does not include the scores of persons working behind the scenes to make this a successful resettlement.

This is a story of only nine of the 136,000 refugees who fled during the evacuation of Vietnam in April 1975.

# 1
# The Vision

The blind pianist . . . softly playing an original composition . . . was inviting us . . . in a tender warm way . . . to a fuller commitment. I heard him . . . half singing . . . yet speaking in a whisper . . . asking us to give up that part of our lives which we had not yet dedicated to the Lord.

I sat in the pew next to my husband, Dale . . . a successful middle-aged businessman . . . holding his hand gently as I examined my life for that one thing I had not given over completely to God.

A cold chill swept through my body as I suddenly remembered a terrifying night . . . the harrowing escape I experienced . . . when the devastating flood spawned by Hurricane Agnes struck without warning. As I struggled frantically to control my two-ton T-Bird automobile being swept away by the raging floodwaters . . . in desperation I cried out to God, "Save me and I'll do anything You ask." God saved me from drowning that night. Then and there I committed my life to Him.

Not long after that I heard Harold Hill . . . a wealthy businessman . . . give his personal testimony. After describing the changes that had taken place in his family life, he prayed for us. As he did, I turned our three children over to God.

A year later, while listening to a soul-searching message on financial resources by Frances Gardner Hunter, I held up my wallet while she prayed. It was at that moment that I dedicated our wealth to God.

And now I hear this blind man asking me to give something more. . . . What have I left to give? . . . I have already given my life, our children, and our money.

The quiet, subtle realization dawned slowly upon me to dedicate our house!

No, not our house! Why, it's the showplace of Owl Valley! Eighteen rooms filled with lovely antiques and mementos from our travels here and abroad. No . . . oh, no! The house . . . our major investment . . . with the barn . . . the horses . . . the meadow with the winding creek. . . .

But the quiet urge persisted. . . .

Reluctantly I wrote "our house" on the small white card the ushers had distributed to each of us that morning in the sanctuary. I told no one of my decision . . . not even my husband.

A week later I shared my secret with Carl . . . my dear quadriplegic confidant. He rejoiced to know that I had dedicated our house to God.

Often during the fourteen months that followed . . . Carl, my precious prayer partner . . . would inquire what the Lord was doing with our house. My answer was always the same . . . "Nothing."

In the early spring, the wife of a prominent pediatrician in our town telephoned to ask if my husband and I would be willing to have our home included in the annual Holiday House tour in December to raise money for a reputable charitable organization.

Of course I was flattered. A worthy cause, I speculated, as I enjoyed another ego trip. Nine hundred, maybe one thousand, ticket holders would walk through our home . . . ooh and aah. . . . But something inside caused me to hesitate. Could this be what the Lord had in mind?

I casually mentioned this invitation to my husband . . . later to each of our children . . . and again at the annual family Easter dinner with my parents. Only negative responses seemed to come through . . . with little or no encouragement from anyone.

By the time the deadline rolled around, I phoned the chairman to say I had decided not to "open our home" although I could not supply a good reason for that decision. She graciously accepted my reply.

In early summer the television screen was crowded with news of the evacuation of Saigon . . . the Vietnamese refugees entering the United States . . . and the reopening of a military base in Pennsylvania as a refugee center. A responsive chord was struck inside me as I watched those nameless, grief-stricken faces.

I volunteered to help with the resettlement program at Fort Indiantown Gap.

My first day at the Gap was a heartbreaking one! I handed out sandwiches, soup, and lemonade to oriental strangers who did not know how to talk my language and were still too shocked to smile. I came home following a ten-hour shift . . . a very disillusioned, discouraged person.

I didn't sleep well that night. . . . A foreboding gloom pervaded the atmosphere. . . . I was restless. . . .

The next day I was riding the tractor . . . mowing the lawn and enjoying these beautiful surroundings. My mind wandered back to our daughter's gorgeous garden reception . . . held here amidst delicate yellow flowers in contrast with velvet green grass. I remembered her as she stood . . . a radiant, beautiful bride beneath the white trellis.

But something slowly began to happen. . . . My daughter's lovely face seemed to phase out of focus in my mind. Her precious image was replaced by those nameless, quiet strangers I had seen at the Gap only the day before. I had a vision of an oriental girl standing on the lawn!

Suddenly . . . above the sound of the tractor humming . . . I heard the Lord say clearly and distinctly . . . "I'm ready now . . . are you?"

He was accepting the commitment I had made to Him fourteen months earlier. He was now ready to use our house!

# 2

# My Favorites

Although I didn't know God's plan for bringing these refugees into my life . . . or what the future held for me . . . I went to my desk where I thoughtfully typed a letter in triplicate . . . a copy to each of our three children and their spouses.

I shared with them some of my experiences as a volunteer working with the refugees . . . and the burden I was beginning to feel. Two important events I did not share with them . . . (1) giving our home to the Lord . . . (2) my vision on the lawn.

I closed my letter by telling them that I had felt led to open our home to a refugee family. I made them aware of my feelings about sharing their bedrooms and bathrooms with total strangers. I was deeply interested in how they felt too. I requested that they share their feelings with me. I assured them this would be only a temporary arrangement . . . this would always be their home!

As I typed, I prayed that the Spirit would guide me and supply the right words . . . also that the children would receive this news graciously and be pleased.

I have two photographs of each of our children on a small antique table at the top of the back stairway . . . one of each of them taken at nine weeks of age in the same dress . . . and a college graduation photo of each. I have developed the rewarding habit of praying for each child every time I walk up those stairs. Sometimes I come up the stairs dozens of times in a day . . . some days much less . . . but I never miss a day praying for our children, Kendra, Jeffrey, and Johnny . . . and their spouses.

# 3
# Waiting

Now that I was convinced that God wanted to use our home . . . I just had to wait for His direction.

I continued my work as a volunteer at Fort Indiantown Gap. Although most of the Gap was restricted and off limits to civilians . . . I soon discovered that I was able to meet some of the right people and get into areas prohibited to others. This enabled me to observe the refugees as they existed day to day under these temporary horrible conditions.

When I arrived at the Gap early in the morning, I saw freshly laundered clothing hanging outside almost every barrack. These industrious Vietnamese were early risers and diligent workers.

I watched as young people by the hundreds learned to play a new American game with a net (volleyball). I saw seventy refugees crowd into a temporary classroom designed to accommodate twenty-five . . . eager to learn everything the American educator would teach them.

I visited the clothing distribution center where every refugee was carefully watched as he chose used clothing . . . all of it American. The Vietnamese are a small and petite people. Soon notices were posted . . . and newspaper dispatches released . . . that only infant, children, and teenage clothing were acceptable. The adult American sizes were just too large.

# 4

# Our First Encounter

I learned of a family of nine through our good neighbors . . . Betty and Bob . . . who had met the father on their first trip to Fort Indiantown Gap. The Vietnamese man . . . working as an interpreter in the Visitor's Center . . . was extremely helpful as Betty and Bob questioned him about an available Vietnamese couple for them to sponsor.

Bob took a picture of this nine member family . . . and gave the photograph to me. When I saw the size of the family I was apprehensive . . . could Dale and I afford to take so many?

But because I was so certain of God's direction . . . I decided to interview them.

Our first meeting had been prearranged. I was scheduled to meet my prospective family at 12:30 at the Visitor's Center. I had been working as a volunteer all morning . . . handing out doughnuts and orange drink . . . but my apprehension grew as I thought of my after-lunch meeting.

How would they look? . . . Would I recognize them from the photo? . . . Could we communicate? . . . Would they like me? . . . Would I like them?

About 12:15 the coordinator came in his car to pick me up and take me to the Center. Although he tried to keep our conversation light and pleasant . . . I felt uneasy.

As we drove to the Center, I saw hundreds and hundreds of refugees waiting in long lines . . . to enter the mess hall . . . the clothing distribution center . . . the makeshift classrooms . . . the health care center . . . and the post exchange.

I wanted to make a good impression. I arranged my hair . . . repaired my makeup . . . as we drove. All the while I was praying . . . silently.

We parked outside the Center. As we followed the white ropes that kept the Vietnamese inside and the Americans outside, I remembered those horrifying stories I had read about the World War II concentration camps.

Outside the Center were long picnic tables full of children with straight black hair . . . eagerly crowding around the American teacher . . . repeating the words she was saying as she held up brightly colored pictures.

"Child," she pronounced slowly and deliberatly . . . as she held up a picture of a solitary child. Her Vietnamese pupils echoed eagerly, "Child." Holding up a picture of a group of children she said, "Children." Her new pupils responded, "Children." I stood quietly and watched. Never before had I observed such an eagerness to learn.

At the desk inside, two Vietnamese men acted as interpreters for the American sponsors coming to interview the refugees. I was advised that no interpreter would be needed . . . the man I was coming to interview could speak English and French well.

A Red Cross volunteer held out a paper cup filled with lemonade in the middle of this stifling hot empty room. I took it, thanked her, tasted it . . . luke warm . . . and continued toward the back of the room where some bare wooden tables and a few chairs stood.

As the coordinator chatted amicably, I kept my eyes glued to the front door. I watched the yellow school bus pull up out front.

School buses were used to transport the 17,000 refugees from one area to another. No Vietnamese were allowed outside the white ropes that surrounded Fort Indiantown Gap.

Several refugees got off the bus as I watched. "Where are Dong and Anh?. . . Will I recognize them?" My eyes riveted on the young couple approaching. She was petite . . . dark and pretty. He was small . . . handsome with a lovely smile and beautiful white teeth.

Suddenly Anh was in my arms . . . sobbing softly . . . with her forehead against my shoulder. Following the proper introductions by our coordinator, I vaguely remember shaking hands with Dong . . . then finding my way back to the group of chairs I had previously arranged.

We sat down and I looked at them closely. She was wearing a dark red, loose-fitting blouse with black slacks. Her hair was short, straight, and very black. Her eyes almost closed as she smiled. She was very neat. I liked her immediately. Her fingernails were perfectly manicured. I wondered how this young refugee mother with five children could have such lovely hands. I later learned that she had gone to the post exchange at the Gap and had purchased a file and nail polish in anticipation of this meeting.

My eyes went to Dong. He sported a blue shirt . . . open at the neck . . . black trousers . . . black shoes. I found out later that he had bought the shirt at the post exchange for this special occasion.

I had so many questions. . . . I wanted so much to help these beautiful people . . . but I was at a loss for words. . . . I couldn't speak.

The coordinator did a good job of interviewing them . . . asking all the right questions. Dong answered in near perfect English, after interpreting each question for Anh.

I remember so clearly Dong saying, "I am surprised that you would want to sponsor my large family." I saw his eyes fill with tears as I answered with all the courage I could muster, "I have a large house."

"What job does your husband have, Mrs. Crist?"

"He's in the dairy business and responsible for milk routes."

"I can help him," Dong replied.

I insisted they both call me Evamae. Dong

pronounced it over and over to Anh until she was able to say quite clearly, "Evamae." That was the first and the last time any of our Vietnamese family ever called me Mrs. Crist.

I described Dale's work and his long hours. . . . I told them of my joy as a homemaker . . . that we both collect antiques . . . Dale enjoys photography . . . gardening rates high on my hobby list . . . I love to read . . . we both enjoy entertaining at home and do a great deal of it . . . and we both love to travel.

Dong and Anh listened attentively.

We talked at length about their five children . . . about Grandmother Le . . . and Vu, Anh's brother who lived with them . . . making nine in the type of extended family for which the Vietnamese are well known.

I shared some of my hopes for their family and what I felt I could do to help them. Dong shared his dreams with me. He was anticipating the day when he could again resume his place as head of his home. During the escape and now as refugees with no country, no family, and few friends, he was looking forward to the time when he could reestablish a home for his family . . . a place to call his own. He talked much about educating his children in America and . . . hopefully . . . encouraging them to return . . . someday . . . as teachers . . . to their native country, Vietnam.

During our discussion I shared some of the things I felt would be beneficial in helping them arrive at a decision that only they could make. . . . Did they really want to become a part of the Crist household?

I laid down some of the ground rules observed in our home . . . no smoking . . . no drinking . . . no profanity . . . mutual respect for each member of the family . . . independence is encouraged . . . but we are closely bonded together . . . we let others know where we are going . . . who we will be with . . . and what time we will return. . . . We support our church . . . with faithful attendance . . . loyalty . . . and money. . . . We are active in volunteer work. . . . We help each other . . . and above all . . . we are part of the family of God!

I paused as he interpreted every word to Anh. "And Dong," I continued, "I have this . . . well, a compulsion . . . you might call it . . . to put everything in its proper place. I simply cannot tolerate anything untidy. I like things neat and orderly. . . . Do you understand, Dong?"

What must they be thinking? With five children could everything be kept in place? . . . Could they fit into a lifestyle like mine? . . . Was this the price they had to pay for their freedom from this refugee center?

Cautiously we were both learning to know each other. At the end of the hour we agreed that I would like to have them live in our home if our church would sponsor them . . . and they would like to live with us even though they had not met my husband.

I told them I would talk to our congregation and would let them know the decision. I gave Dong our telephone number . . . and asked him to phone me in three days . . . on Friday night at 7:00 p.m. I walked to the public telephone with him . . . gave him a dime . . . showed him how to use it. I also taught him how to call me collect.

As I prepared to leave them, Anh put her arms around me and said something in her native tongue. I looked toward Dong for an interpretation. "Anh said to tell you that even if you do not sponsor our family she will never forget you."

I looked at her through tears and watched her wipe her eyes with a clean white handkerchief.

They were both extremely gracious as they waved good-bye, smiled, walked out of the room . . . and boarded that same yellow bus.

The coordinator drove me back to my volunteer job and somehow I got through the afternoon. I could hardly wait to get home to tell my husband all about what had happened that day.

After listening to my lengthy enthusiastic report all during dinner, he asked one slow, deliberate question. "Do you like them, Evamae?" Eagerly I replied, "Honey, I love them."

I knew the Lord was guiding all these developments as they unfolded. We had just finished dinner when our assistant pastor phoned. After giving him a full report of my volunteer job at Indiantown Gap that day he asked, "Can you come to an emergency meeting tomorrow night at the church? Our district representative is coming to talk to us about resettling a Vietnamese family." I promised him I'd be in his office the next evening at 7:30. All the while he was talking I was saying inside myself, "Thank you, Jesus. Praise the Lord!"

I knew then that the Lord was beginning to put this whole thing together!

# 5

# A Double Portion of Strength

I went to the meeting in our assistant pastor's office. Arden, chairman of the Witness Commission, John, our district representative, and Ralph, director of Special Ministries, were waiting when I walked in. Ralph began: "John is here from the district office to explain the mechanics of sponsoring a refugee family. We'll hear his presentation . . . discuss it . . . then decide whether we should present the idea to the congregation on Sunday morning. John, proceed."

I interrupted. "May I say something first?" The three men nodded.

I began my story by telling them how I had dedicated our house to the Lord more than a year before. I told them that a month ago He had told me He was ready to use it now for a Vietnamese family. I shared with them the experience I had the day before . . . meeting Dong and Anh . . .

how much I wanted to help them get out of the Gap to begin a new life.

At that point of the meeting . . . my husband walked into the office. I had written him a note at home asking for his support.

In tears I told them how very much I desired the help of our church in sponsoring this large family. With my husband present to support me, I added quickly, "Dale and I have decided that we will sponsor them on our own . . . if the church doesn't care to help."

I was only able to make such a sweeping statement because I claimed that precious promise, "I can do all things through Christ who strengthens me."

When I finished . . . there was complete silence in that office.

Suddenly the men began talking . . . each offering support and encouragement to Dale and to me. Following the discussion, we all agreed that Arden would present this idea to our congregation on Sunday morning . . . asking if they would be willing to sponsor a Vietnamese family . . . regardless of size.

As sponsor we had to assure the United States government officials at Fort Indiantown Gap that we would assume full responsibility for . . . finding suitable housing . . . adequate employment . . . proper schooling for the children . . . and offer the family moral support.

I left out one important point. I did not tell these men that Dong was going to call me the very next night for a decision. I was so positive that this was the direction the Lord had for my life that I was ready to take on all the responsibility for these nine displaced persons . . . even if my church voted against it!

The phone rang promptly at seven o'clock on Friday evening. It was Dong calling me collect as I had instructed him to do.

"Dong, after much prayer and discussion, Dale and I have decided that we will sponsor your family."

A long silence followed. . . . Finally I heard him respond with, "Thank you very much, Evamae."

Soon Dong was able to talk and he said, "Evamae, Anh would like to talk with you." I was astounded! On Wednesday she was not able to speak a word of English and now she wanted to talk to me!

"Evamae, I am so happy to know you," she said haltingly in perfect English. She had memorized a whole sentence just for me. How thoughtful she was!

"Dong, Dale wants to meet you and we both want to see your children."

"Yes, Evamae, yes, yes."

"We will drive up to see you. Will you come to the Visitor's Center on Sunday afternoon at four o'clock?"

"Yes, Evamae, yes. We will come to the Visitor's Center on Sunday with all our children. Thank you very much, Evamae."

# 6

# The People Say Yes

Sunday morning finally arrived . . . and my husband and I were seated in our usual pew near the front of the church. Following the morning service, a special congregational meeting was called by our moderator. Arden gave a beautiful presentation . . . outlining the need to help resettle the refugees . . . explaining the availability of the Crist home . . . as well as the responsibilities our church would be expected to assume.

During the discussion period that followed, several members asked intelligent questions regarding housing, employment, health, and financing. The vote was taken. "All in favor of our congregation sponsoring a Vietnamese family . . . regardless of size . . . will please stand."

Hesitatingly, I turned around to look . . . and every member of our congregation was on his feet! "Praise the Lord! Praise God!" I said to myself.

The meeting adjourned.... Suddenly I was surrounded with dozens of people . . . all hugging me. I felt such love! I kept whispering, "Thank you, Jesus."

I immediately made arrangements for some friends to go along to Indiantown Gap that afternoon . . . to meet the refugee family. "We'll leave the parking lot at three o'clock," I told them.

By three o'clock it was pouring rain . . . but the three-car caravan proceeded to the Gap as planned.

What a mob scene we encountered when we arrived at the Visitor's Center! Hordes of refugees . . . all looking for their prospective sponsors . . . dozens of American families looking for their Vietnamese families. I had an advantage over many other prospective sponsors there that Sunday afternoon. . . . I had met Dong and Anh four days earlier.

Fourteen of us from our church pushed our way slowly through the crowd to one area of the room that seemed a little less congested. I looked around anxiously . . . hoping to spot Dong and Anh in that teeming throng.

Just then I saw them walking toward me. Dong was carrying a little child, Anh grasped another, and a tall young man was following them . . . leading a small boy on his right and another on his left. I hurried toward them.

Anh hugged me and broke into tears. She and Dong both must have realized that this could be the beginning of a new life for them . . . their first hope since they left Saigon. Because of the size of their family, most sponsors skipped right over their names.

Dong introduced me to each of his children in that maddening mass. It was difficult to hear and to speak but I did my best. I met Phuong, a two-year-old girl . . . Nguyen, a four-year-old girl . . . Viet, a five-year-old boy . . . Quyen, a seven-year-old boy, Vu, Anh's twenty-year-old brother. Dong quickly informed me that his mother-in-law and Baby John had remained in the barracks because of the severity of the rainstorm.

I took Anh's hand and slowly led her around the circle, giving her an opportunity to meet each of the persons from my church. At times Anh sobbed uncontrollably. Even though we were unable to communicate with words, I saw so much love as each person hugged Anh and welcomed Dong and all the children with the candy they had thoughtfully brought with them.

It was so hot I could hardly breathe. Dale suggested that we go out to an adjoining room to take pictures and to become better acquainted. My nervous conversation continued but there was little response. How frustrating it was for me . . . being unable to make these people understand.

I told Dong that our church members had voted unanimously to sponsor his family and that these people . . . representing the church . . . had come to welcome them. Dong gathered his family around him and explained to them in their native language why we were there.

Finally Dong and I were able to find a small table in the corner. Together we began the detailed task of filling out the governmental forms as the first official step in refugee resettlement.

An hour later we were saying good-bye and rushing through the rain to our cars. We watched our refugee family board a yellow school bus to take them back to Area Five where their barrack was located.

Now I must begin the tedious preparations of our home to prepare it for our influx of guests!

# 7

# Five Hundred Every December

An important event in the Crist family is our annual Christmas card. Each year we have a current photograph taken for the front of our greeting. Inside we show the photos of all the previous years. . . . This year we mailed out an accumulation of thirty years of photographs . . . one for each year beginning with our wedding picture.

I mailed one of our Christmas cards to Dong and Anh . . . that rainy Sunday night . . . along with an affectionate letter . . . expressing my hopes and dreams for their family. I let them know that I wanted to help them establish a new life . . . and assured them that I didn't want to make Americans out of them.

I hoped Dong and Anh could begin to feel a part of the family on the greeting . . . as they watched it grow with each successive card . . . from births through weddings.

# 8
# Taking Inventory

Early Monday morning the telephone rang. It was Arden . . . who had given a beautiful presentation the day before in church. He had also gone along with us to the Gap that same afternoon to meet Dong's family. He was calling to assure me of the full cooperation of the church and of his commission . . . of which I am a member. He asked about my immediate needs and I told him I had none.

Mentally I began taking inventory . . . plenty of room in our home . . . eight bedrooms and four bathrooms . . . plenty of sheets, blankets, towels, and washcloths . . . a cupboard full of canned goods . . . a freezer packed with frozen foods and meats. I could think of absolutely nothing that I needed to welcome the Vietnamese family into our home.

"We are all praying for you," Arden said. That

reminded me . . . I did need their prayers . . . their encouragement . . . their support . . . I told him. Little did I realize that Monday morning how much support I'd need in the days ahead.

Before he hung up he asked, "When do you think you'll be getting the family?"

"Till we get through all the government's red tape, I imagine it will be a couple weeks, Arden."

"Keep in touch," he said . . . and then added, "God bless you, Evamae," . . . and hung up.

That same night during dinner my husband and I discussed the psychological preparation we would have to make. He pointed out that I no longer should come down to prepare breakfast in my robe . . . but would need to be fully dressed each morning. I wondered out loud if he would continue his habit of falling asleep in the den every evening while he read the paper in his favorite chair.

We agreed to support each other . . . to provide the little reminders that would make for smoother sailing.

I wonder now why neither of us considered . . . the staggering stacks of laundry . . . the extensive food preparation . . . the excessive use of water . . . the resulting cesspool overflow . . . the transportation problems . . . the physical stamina required . . . the tremendous financial responsibility . . . the overwhelmingly high food costs . . . the cultural differences . . . the language barrier . . . and the inability to communicate.

Oblivious to all these obstacles . . . we stumbled on blindly . . . certain of only one thing . . . we both knew this project was God's will!

# 9
# Why Are Folks So Cruel?

I soon discovered that not everyone was as enthusiastic about resettling these Vietnamese refugees as I. Until I was absolutely certain they were coming to live with us, I made no mention of it to anyone. . . . There seemed to be so many technicalities. When I was sure . . . I began sharing my good news.

I saw my friend's car approaching as I was kneeling in the flower bed . . . pulling weeds. I jumped up and ran toward him.

Panting and out of breath, I ran up to his car as he pulled into our driveway. I asked, "Guess who's coming to our house for dinner?"

"What did you say?" he asked.

I repeated the question. "Guess who's coming to our house for dinner?"

"I don't understand," he answered.

I began telling my story . . . carefully omitting

the part where I dedicated our house to the Lord. I described my volunteer work at Fort Indiantown Gap . . . my interview with Dong and Anh . . . meeting the children. I told him we were expecting nine Vietnamese refugees to move in with us soon.

No answer . . . just silence accompanied his look of utter disdain. He slammed his car into reverse . . . pressed hard on the accelerator . . . the tires squealed . . . tiny pebbles flew back across the lawn. . . . He pulled away . . . leaving me standing there alone. . . .

I was stunned! He always seemed so special. . . . He was my friend . . . one who cares about us, the children, and the garden. He is a great traveler . . . eager to share with us the delights of his latest cruise or flight.

I stood there dumbfounded. Could this be the same man that I have known and appreciated for so many years? Why would he react like that?

Dejectedly I walked back to my pachysandra bed with a slow, dull ache in my stomach. The longer I weeded, the more I began to worry. What if my neighbors rejected our new family? What if my friends would not accept them? Was I making a mistake? Was it too late to back out now?

Feverishly I pulled weeds! Suddenly a warm calm came over me as I remembered Christ's words, "I was a stranger and you took me in."

I worked in my flower garden all afternoon . . . enjoying the hot summer sun and an occasional sip of iced tea. All the while I was making plans for our new family!

When my husband came home for dinner that evening, he was hardly inside the door when I told him about the encounter with my friend. He listened to my story . . . looked at me sympathetically . . . and said, "If you think that's bad, just wait till you hear what happened to me."

"Tell me, tell me," I pleaded quickly.

"I couldn't wait to get to work this morning to tell everyone that we are inviting a Vietnamese family into our home. When I stepped out of my car in the company parking lot, I told the first man I saw. You know what he said? He looked me straight in the eyes and said, 'Boy, you're insane.' It nearly wiped me out. I didn't tell another soul."

I could hardly believe my ears. Is this what we could expect from those we always felt had really cared about us?

I served dinner . . . but as we ate together . . . a certain indefinable sadness pervaded our cozy kitchen lighted only by the candles on the table. We both tried to be cheerful . . . but our underlying uncertainty could not be denied.

Later that night in bed my husband held me and asked, "Do you think we're making a mistake?"

I whispered softly the same verse that had provided so much encouragement to me earlier that day. "I was a stranger and you took me in." Apparently that was the only assurance he needed. Moments later he was sleeping soundly.

The next morning I kept my regularly scheduled appointment with the hairdresser. I shared my good news with her . . . and the other Saturday morning regulars in the salon. They had a multitude of questions . . . but the one that persisted was, "Why are you doing this?"

Before I could answer adequately, the conversation shifted to food. They all asked questions. . . . What do they eat? . . . Do I know how to cook Oriental food? . . . How can I feed so many? . . . Would I allow the Vietnamese to cook? . . . Do I like their food? . . . How long would they be living with me? . . . Do they eat lots of fish? . . . Isn't rice their favorite dish?

Situated on the road home from the beauty shop is an interesting little country general store. The proprietor had always been kind to me . . . and went out of his way to honor my special requests. For our frequent corn roasts he was always able to furnish bushels of fresh sweet corn on the cob. For our parties in the barn he was always able to provide the juiciest apples and the best watermelons.

Excitedly I entered his store . . . eager to tell him about the Vietnamese family we were expecting soon. I was sure he would share my happiness.

There were other customers in the store as I entered. I waited my turn in line. My grocer friend listened with interest . . . but was not as enthusiastic as I had hoped he would be. I inquired about large, commercial-size cans of fruits and vegetables as I mentally was figuring out the cost of our meals.

He walked around the store with me . . . pointing out some of his best buys. I told him I would be preparing approximately thirty meals per day. "What can I serve, Mr. Smith, that will be nutritious but not costly?" I asked.

Just then a man standing nearby said, "I have a good idea what you could give them." Eager for all the free advice I could get, I looked toward him and asked, "What?"

"A large dose of strychnine," he answered.

In tears . . . I ran from the store.

Driving home was so difficult . . . with weeping eyes. I prayed out loud as I drove slowly. "Please, precious Jesus, help me. I can't cope with all this adverse public reaction. Please assure me we are doing the right thing. Please let me know this is Your will.

The same still calmness gradually came over me again . . . warm and reassuring. "I was a stranger and you took me in."

Following my third affirmation within the last twenty-four hours, I was certain I was following the direction of the Lord! With that I put public sentiment out of my mind for good . . . and continued my final preparations for their arrival.

# 10

# They're Really Coming!

I was peeling potatoes when the phone rang. I wiped my hands and answered.

"May I speak with E-v-a-m" the girl began spelling.

I knew this was the call I had been awaiting. I almost shouted into the phone, interrupting her, "Is this Indiantown Gap calling?"

The girl identified herself as a Church World Service representative but in my excitement I didn't hear her name. "You may pick up the Dong Nguyen family at the Debarkation Center anytime after 8:00 a.m. tomorrow morning."

Frantically, I tried to remember what my husband had said that morning when he left for work. Each morning, in anticipation of this call, we would remind each other of our commitments for that day. We wanted to go together to the Gap to pick up our family.

"My husband has an important meeting tomorrow morning so we can't get to the Center before 3:00 in the afternoon. Will that be satisfactory?"

"Certainly," I heard her answer. "I'll tell the family to expect you at three o'clock. Do you know how to reach Fort Indiantown Gap?"

"Yes, thank you. I've been there many times."

"Thank you, Mrs. Crist."

I hung up the phone and ran from my house . . . down the front steps . . . across the road . . . into the home of Betty and Bob, our dear neighbors . . . who had made the initial contact with Dong at the Gap.

"They're coming tomorrow . . . they're coming tomorrow," I shouted almost hysterically. Betty rushed out of her kitchen . . . hugged me . . . and together we wept tears of joy! She and I had waited sixteen days for that phone call.

I rushed back home as soon as I was able. I called my husband's office and shared the good news with him! He, too, was overjoyed!

That night was the last time we had dinner alone at home for a long time. Little did we realize then how much we appreciated the privacy and intimacy of our candlelight dinners . . . which we were about to give up.

# 11

# Welcome Home

The ringing of the telephone interrupted my lunch. I was surprised to hear Dong's voice. "Evamae?"

"Yes," I answered.

"When do you come for us?"

"Didn't that girl tell you, Dong? Dale and I will be there at three o'clock to get you."

"Nobody tell us when you come."

"Oh, Dong, I'm so sorry. We'll see you at three today."

"Thank you very much, Evamae."

I was so disappointed. Why hadn't she told him what time to expect us? Waiting all morning with all those children . . . maybe they thought we had changed our minds . . . doubts must have arisen. I am sure they realized that their entire future depended upon their release from that Refugee Center.

I dressed as soon as I had finished lunch. When I was ready to go, I made one quick trip over the whole house to make certain I hadn't forgotten anything.

I went to the third floor . . . into the master bedroom I had reserved for Dong and Anh. Everything in place . . . a television set so that Dong could watch the news . . . a new outfit for each child was carefully arranged on the bed . . . a crib for Baby John . . . a basin . . . baby soap . . . talcum powder . . . Kleenex . . . crib sheets and blankets.

Then into the girls bedroom . . . decorated in blue with gaily flowered wallpaper . . . a white rocking chair trimmed in pink . . . just right for two little girls.

Into the bathroom . . . all fixtures gleaming brightly . . . freshly laundered towels folded neatly . . . a good supply of toothpaste, soap, tissue, deodorant . . . had I forgotten anything?

I came down to the second-floor bedrooms and bath . . . the brown masculine room with twin beds would be perfect for Vu and Quyen . . . through the yellow bathroom . . . into Grandmother Le's room with the lovely white draperies and woolen carpet. All was in readiness!

As I closed the back door behind me . . . I asked God one last time, "Please, God, make sure I can handle it."

I met my husband at his business and slid into the station wagon beside him. It was a beautiful summer day. We drove with the windows down . . . the fresh clean air blowing my hair. I was so happy . . . such exhilaration!

A deep sense of fulfillment came over me . . . accepting this responsibility had given me a quiet peace . . . yet it presented a tremendous challenge.

The prospect of having five children in our home thrilled me! I hadn't been around youngsters for years. Our youngest son was already twenty-four years old!

As we drove I needed all the reassurances my husband generously offered. Yes, we were doing the right thing. . . . Yes, he was sure I could handle it. . . . No, we weren't making a mistake. . . . Yes, of course it will work out.

The sign read "Fort Indiantown Gap—Next Right." We turned in, entered the camp through the main gate, and continued slowly down the hot macadam road . . . careful to stop at every guard post along the way to the Debarkation Center. Each time the Military Police waved us through.

Dale swung the station wagon around the corner of a huge shabby white building . . . and there they stood. I could hardly believe what I saw! There were all nine of them . . . all their earthly possessions in one big pile.

Dong and Anh waved excitedly as I jumped from the car before it had come to a complete stop. The white ropes were still separating us . . . but Anh stretched her arms out over them . . . and we embraced. I shook hands with Dong.

Immediately, as if on cue, the children began waving and repeating over and over, "Evamae, Evamae, Evamae." Dong had taught them to pronounce my name perfectly. Even precious little Phuong who was just two years old said it correctly. How hard this family tried! How conscientious they were!

Then I saw Grandmother Le for the first time. She was small, very thin with wide brown sad eyes and long straight hair. I wanted her to know how glad I was to see her. I reached out to hug her and as I did I fell over the ropes that were separating us. Dale and Dong somehow caught me . . . but my poise was shattered.

I was surprised at the complete silence of all these people. I kept on chatting nervously but there was no response . . . and I felt uneasy. I had to remember that only Dong could understand what I was saying.

A stack of pillows and blankets were piled on the ground beside this little group huddled together. Dong told us the bedclothing had to be returned to the Orientation Center. Dale, Dong, Vu, and I walked up the hot macadam road . . . each carrying an armload of pillows and blankets. We checked them in to an Army sergeant who appeared to be completely disinterested. I was so excited with my new family that I expected everyone else to feel the same.

Another officer carefully checked through the stack of personal papers Dong was carrying in a brown envelope. Each member of the family had been assigned a Social Security number . . . photographed and fingerprinted . . . given a registered alien number . . . and had received the necessary inoculations from the United States Department of Health.

The officer handed everything back to Dong

. . . except the white cards showing they were registered aliens. These cards he handed to me . . . just as though they could now be considered my prisoners. I could not tolerate the insensitivity of this officer. I immediately handed them over to Dong . . . right in front of the officer . . . who looked surprised. I was eager to restore human dignity to these displaced persons who already had endured so much persecution.

Finally we were cleared . . . ready to begin packing the station wagon. I looked at the pile of baggage which represented everything in this world the family owned. Among the brown cardboard cartons I saw a plastic scrub bucket . . . and a baby's plastic bathtub.

A huge cardboard box was filled with Pampers . . . given by the United States government to Baby John . . . along with a one-month supply of canned formula.

I was impressed as I watched the children help Dong and Dale pack the station wagon . . . each seemed so eager to do his part. When all was packed, eleven of us crowded into the wagon . . . anxious for the one-hour trip that would take them to their new home in southeastern Pennsylvania.

On the way the children were animated and talkative. I was sure they were talking about us. Much to my surprise . . . when I asked Dong to interpret what they were saying . . . he would answer, "Look at the bridge. . . . I see a tree. . . . I hear an airplane. . . . I'm too hot."

Before we reached home the three youngest children had fallen asleep. I was glad . . . for I had planned a big homecoming garden party for that evening. . . . I knew the naps would benefit the children.

We crossed the bridge. . . . There was our home! I pointed it out to the family and said, "Welcome home." Dong looked at the house and said, "Very beautiful." Immediately Anh repeated, "Very beautiful."

After parking in the driveway, Dale opened the car doors. The children jumped from the car and ran down through the yard. Dong told us it was the first time they had ever seen this much grass. Weeks later he told us stories of their life in the crowded city of Saigon that brought tears to our eyes . . . and tugged at our hearts.

I was surprised that our new family was much more interested in the yard than the house. Although I had the grass carefully mowed . . . and the flower beds meticulously manicured . . . my real efforts had gone into preparing our home for our new family.

The children soon spied my pet ducks down by the creek that runs through the yard. Dale had given me a dozen ducks for Easter . . . but only nine had survived. Dong laughed when he pointed out, "Nine ducks, nine refugees." I smiled as I looked directly toward him and said, "You are home now, Dong, no longer a refugee." The word refugee was not used among us after that.

Eventually we all got around to coming inside the house. I took them on a quick tour of our home. . . . pointing out only the most essential things. Although I suggested who should sleep in each bedroom, I left the final decision up to them. Their quarters included four bedrooms with six beds and two private bathrooms. Suddenly our home did not seem as spacious as it had before.

Every word that I said had to be interpreted by Dong to his family. What effort it took to carry on a conversation like this. Could I cope? I was trusting God to take me through. It was a grave situation for me to handle and I knew I couldn't do it alone.

Our friends began arriving at 6:30 for the welcoming party . . . each bringing some part of the meal. The same persons who went to Indiantown Gap two Sundays before to meet the family were the invited dinner guests that evening. I had made name tags for easy identification.

It was then that I discovered what a real barrier our language had created. All of us were eager to reach out in love to this family . . . but communication was so difficult. However, we soon discovered that smiles, hugs, and kisses were understood in both languages. As we sat on lawn chairs around the fireplace that night under the trees, I felt a real sense of well-being and I was sure we had made the right decision.

We closed our bedroom door that night for the first in a long time. We wanted to share our home but also maintain some privacy.

A crying child awakened us the next morning. Dale rolled over and commented, "I hope this doesn't happen often." Little did he know how many times in the future his sleep would be interrupted by the sounds of children crying.

Although hundreds of meals have been prepared and served in our kitchen I will never forget that first breakfast. All at once there were eleven of us in the kitchen ready for breakfast. I debated quickly and silently with myself. "Shall I prepare and serve breakfast? Shall I show them how? Shall I let them do it their way? What shall I do?"

Slowly I began a very arduous task. I opened the refrigerator, removed a quart of fresh orange juice, went to the cupboard, and took out a juice glass. They stood quietly . . . watching me as I poured. It was as if I was on exhibition and I felt uneasy.

I opened the bread drawer, took out a loaf of bread, and dropped two slices into the toaster. The children had never seen an automatic toaster so you can imagine their surprise when the toast popped up.

I went again to the refrigerator and got out butter and jelly. Then to the cupboard once more where I took out a small plate for the toast . . . and placed it on the table. Next I took a cereal bowl from the cupboard, went to the lazy Susan full of cereal, picked out a favorite, poured it into a bowl, opened the refrigerator, took out milk, poured it on, added sugar, and set it on the table. How strange this must all seem to them, I thought.

I approached the refrigerator again . . . but stopped . . . No, I decided . . . no scrambled eggs this morning. I have my hands full already.

I showed them a drawer full of silverware . . . took out a spoon and a knife. I removed a paper napkin from the holder. They watched closely as Dong interpreted each word I was saying.

What effort that had taken! I began to experience my first feelings of discouragement.

I looked over at Dale who had propped himself against the dishwasher and had watched this whole procedure in silence. With a look of bewilderment he threw his hands up in the air and calmly announced, "I'm getting out of here," and promptly walked out of the kitchen and left for work without a bite of breakfast.

I wanted to cry out and beg him not to leave me here alone to cope with all this. But instead I whispered another short prayer to God who had directed me into this path. "Please help me . . . thank You."

At that moment beautiful little two-year-old Phuong walked over to me, took one of my hands into both of her little chubby ones, and said with a big grin, "Evamae, Evamae, Evamae." It was the only English word she knew.

# 12

# In Christ There Is No Far East

What a fine processional it was . . . down the center aisle of our lovely church . . . coming toward me as I stood at the front . . . a lavaliere microphone in my hand.

The church organist was playing softly "In Christ There Is No East or West" as our Vietnamese family came forward to meet . . . for the first time . . . the members of the church who had voted unanimously to sponsor them.

I introduced each one individually as they reached the chancel steps. "I am happy to present to you our . . . I mean . . . your family. This is seven-year-old Quyen."

Quyen stepped closer and spoke into the mike, "Good morning."

"Here is five-year-old Viet."

"Good morning."

"Four-year-old Nguyen."

"Good morning."

"And two-year-old Phuong."

Phuong approached the microphone but instead of saying, "Good morning," as we had rehearsed so thoroughly the previous day, she reached up to take the mike from my hand. "Phuong, will you say good morning to your new friends?" I pleaded. . . . Nothing. . . . At that moment . . . as if on cue . . . Nguyen walked back to the mike and said, "Good morning," . . . as if to help her little sister out of a predicament.

"This is Grandmother Le and Baby John," I said.

Not a sound . . . just a nod.

"This is beautiful Anh." Anh looked toward Dong . . . walked to the microphone and said, "Good morning" . . . with much shyness and her ingratiating smile.

"We're missing one," I continued. "Vu is ill and is home in bed . . . and this is Dong."

I handed the mike to Dong . . . and with his heart overflowing with gratitude he began, "I am very happy to be here with my family today. I am very grateful to God, to the United States of America, to President Ford, to you people here at this church who are my sponsors, and to Dale and Evamae. . . ."

I didn't hear the rest of Dong's thanksgiving. . . .

Our church members began to organize various committees to help meet the needs of Dong and his family. There was a committee for education . . . a committee for clothing . . . a committee for transportation . . . a committee for food processing.

English classes . . . taught by several public schoolteachers of our congregation . . . were started at once and held regularly. Drivers came promptly and regularly to transport the family to and from their lessons.

Bushels of fresh fruits and vegetables were canned and frozen by volunteers in the church . . . and stored until needed by our Vietnamese family.

Many members of the church came to our home . . . to visit and to fellowship with our new family . . . bringing with them fresh produce from their gardens along with pies, bananas, meat, and homemade bread.

As I watched one car after another . . . week after week . . . pull out of our driveway . . . following a satisfying visit with their new Oriental friends . . . I was reminded of the advice Apostle Peter gave us: "Use hospitality one to another without grudging."

I praised the Lord for this congregational support!

# 13

# Please Pass the Meat Loaf

The family was not with us very long before I felt a need to teach them some of our eating patterns which contrast so strongly with their table customs. Deliberately . . . but cautiously . . . I planned my strategy . . . at night in bed . . . which was the only time my husband and I could be alone together. With five children and six adults in our home . . . our quiet times alone became almost nonexistent.

My husband rejected the idea of changing their mealtime customs. "But," I pleaded, "I just want to help them adjust to life in their new country."

Following a prolonged discussion in which we examined my motivation, we decided to put our plan into action the very next evening at dinner.

Because it was one of Dong's favorites, I chose to serve meat loaf the night of our first lesson in

American table etiquette. As I was preparing it, I remembered Vu and how he had served everyone the last time I made a ham loaf. Good natured Vu . . . always helpful . . . always ready to assist . . . helped himself to a slice . . . then took a slice for each member of the family . . . reaching around the table to serve everyone. With his long arms he was able to reach from one end of the table to the other. Although this is entirely proper and even expected of a host in Vietnam, I felt I would do them a favor to teach them our way of doing things.

How can I best handle this, I wondered?

Immediately following our family prayer together . . . during which we held hands . . . I announced, "Tonight we are going to have our first lesson in American dining." Each listened intently as Dong interpreted every word I said.

"The first thing we want to learn is to pass everything to the left . . . so let's begin."

A solemn silence settled over the table. . . . I wondered if I was making a mistake. . . . I am only trying to help them, I rationalized . . . as I passed the basket of hot rolls to Grandmother Le . . . seated on my immediate left. She graciously helped herself . . . and was just ready to serve Viet when she remembered . . . smiled at me . . . and passed the basket to him. Viet took a roll and passed the basket to Quyen . . . to Vu . . . to Dale . . . to Dong . . . to Phuong . . . to Nguyen . . . and to Anh.

Next I passed the butter . . . then the pineapple preserves . . . and followed the same procedure. Meanwhile the food was getting cold. . . .

I was concerned . . . but I persisted.

We lingered long at the table that night. . . . It was a great learning experience for all of us! As I removed the plates from the table before serving dessert, I chanted over and over audibly, "Serve from left, take away right . . . serve from left, take away right."

Following dessert I continued our educational experiment with the children. As I held up each piece of silverware I pronounced it distinctly . . . and the children repeated after me. When we left the table . . . Vu, Grandmother Le, Quyen, Viet, and Nguyen could not only recognize . . . but could pronounce "knife, fork, spoon, and napkin."

When I walked into the kitchen I discovered a pot of rice on the stove that had not been served at dinner. I called Anh from the patio. As she looked at it she laughed and said, "Learning so difficult . . . I forget rice."

I thought to myself, "Tomorrow I'll teach the children to say, 'Please pass the butter.' Glass and cup will have to wait until next week!"

# 14
# The Golden Hammer

I waited until I felt certain that he would be home. I dialed his number. He answered. "Walt, this is Evamae Crist. I need help."

"Sure, what can I do for you?"

Discreetly and with caution, I explained how hard I had tried to find employment for Vu . . . Anh's twenty-year old brother . . . who had an inexhaustible appetite . . . and too much leisure time on his hands. My friend was a busy electrician with several trucks and many employees. I was hoping he could use Vu as a helper.

"Well, Evie, things are slow right now. In fact, I just had to lay off another man. But I tell you what I can do for you. I can use him down at the Public Water Works." I learned later that my friend was Borough Council President and the Water Works was a federally funded project.

"Oh, thank you, Walt. You don't know how

much I appreciate this."

"Tell him I'll come by to pick him up at 7:15 tomorrow morning. After that could you take him back and forth to work?"

"Sure, Walt, and . . . thank you so much!"

I ran upstairs to Vu's room and stood in the doorway . . . beaming . . . eager to tell him the good news. He was lying on his bed . . . beside him a tape recorder played his native Vietnamese songs. I don't think a day ever passed that he didn't play those tapes. I often sensed his homesickness by the faraway look in his eyes.

"Vu," I said excitedly, "I've found a job for you. My friend will hire you and you will start tomorrow morning."

"What job, Evamae?" Vu asked. It suddenly occurred to me that I hadn't asked what kind of work Vu would be doing. I was so happy with the prospect of Vu having something to occupy his time that I was willing to settle for anything.

The next morning I packed a nice lunch for Vu. At 7:15 he and I were in the driveway waiting for my friend. I noticed Vu was wearing sandals. He ought to wear something more protective for work . . . I thought . . . but then remembered that he had only one pair of shoes.

Walt pulled into the driveway . . . I introduced Vu . . . and off they went.

A great burden had been lifted and I felt great!

At noon the telephone rang and I answered. It was Vu calling. I asked him how things were going and what kind of work he was doing. He answered, "I cut the tree." I remembered he was wearing only sandals. "Please, dear Jesus, keep

Vu safe and protect him," I prayed.

That evening Vu talked much about his new job. Manual labor was new to him. I was wondering if he could handle it. In Vietnam he was a student . . . having finished two years of law school preparing to be a lawyer.

One morning as I drove him to work, Vu told me he was invited to go along home with his boss that evening for dinner. When he returned home much later that night . . . he was carrying a gift that his boss had given him. He proudly unwrapped his package. There were two new dictionaries . . . one translating English into Vietnamese . . . the other translating Vietnamese into English.

In the front of each book there was an inscription which read, "To Vu, the Golden Hammer." I still don't know its meaning. But I do know those dictionaries were indispensable from that day on!

*The Owl Valley house and grounds Evamae Crist dedicated to the Lord.*

*Evamae and Phuong at the fair*

*Dale and Viet in the den*

*Anh accompanies Viet, Nguyen, and Quyen to their first day of school.*

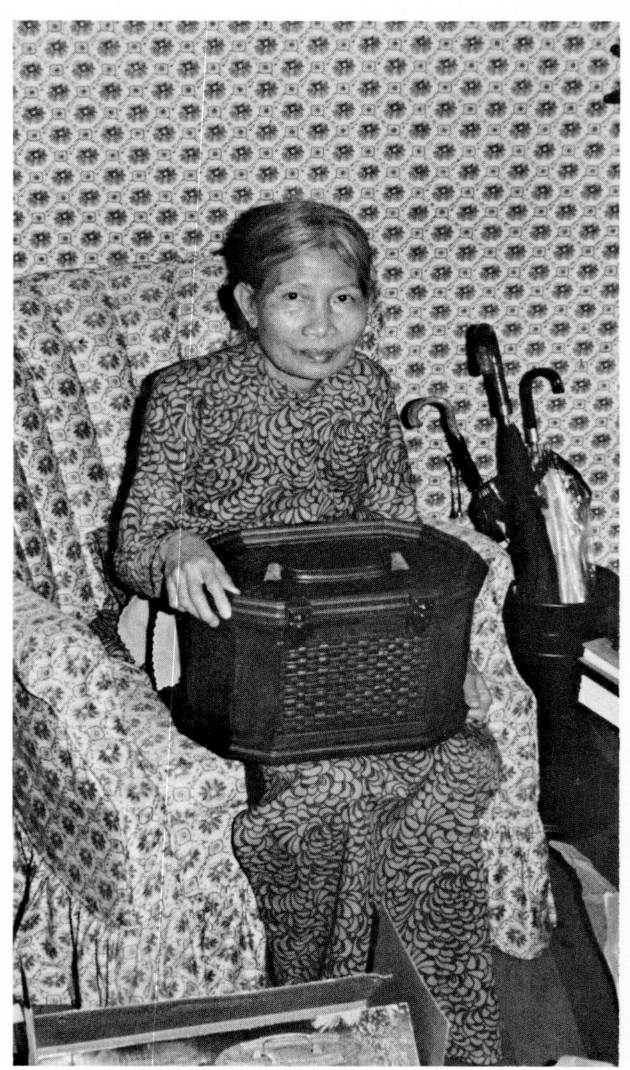

*Grandmother Le receives a sewing box for Christmas.*

*The children at breakfast*

*The dedication of Baby John*

*Anh, Viet, Dong, Quyen, and Phuong opening Christmas presents.*

Dong's Christmas gift for Dale and Evamae

Anh and Dong at a New Year's party

*Author Evamae and Dale*

*Son Jeffrey Dale and Edith*

*Daughter Kendra Eve and Bob*

*Son Johnny Dale and Anne*

# 15

# Whatsoever Things Are Honest

I appreciated the careful honesty of our Vietnamese guests.

Our church congregation had been generously supplying the clothing needs of the family. They had been made aware of the needs as well as the sizes. I tried hard to protect the dignity of Dong's family. When a box of used clothing came to our home, I always insisted that they take it upstairs to try things on . . . in the privacy of their own rooms.

One generous young mother brought a large box overflowing with children's clothing . . . along with a few accessories for Anh. I noticed a pretty brown pocketbook . . . but I had never seen Anh carry a bag when she went out.

Anh anxiously took the big box . . . went upstairs . . . with all the children and Grandmother following. They were so excited . . . it reminded me of Christmas!

In just a few minutes Anh was calling me as she ran down the stairs. She hurried toward me in the kitchen . . . clutching some paper money in her hand. As she gave it to me, she said, "I found this in pocketbook." I stood . . . silent . . . unable to think of any proper response . . . except, "Thank you, Anh."

In the middle of my kitchen I stood holding the money while I praised the Lord for Anh's honesty. Their needs were so great . . . they had so little . . . yet Anh returned those seven dollars.

I immediately phoned the young mother who had shared the box of clothing with us. After I had described the incident to her, she said, "Just keep the money and use it to get something they need."

No wonder Dale and I never worried about the safety and privacy of our home as we continued to pursue our busy social schedule.

# 16

# No One Warned Me

A meeting of all sponsors was scheduled for 9:15 on a Thursday morning. It was already in progress when I entered the room. My eyes slowly took in the group seated around the long conference table.

Who are these people? . . . What kind of person decides to become a sponsor? . . . What are their motivations? . . . What makes them care so deeply? . . . Is it worth all the risks? . . . Did they feel they had made a wise decision? . . . Would they do it all over again? . . . Why are there more men here than women?

I listened intently as each sponsor described the problems involved. . . . It's tough trying to rent an apartment to accommodate seven persons. . . . Can rice be purchased in large quantities? . . . Is your principal aware of the foreign students entering your school district this fall?

. . . How can you find a job if you can't speak the language? . . . How do you cope with homesickness? . . . Are there any medical provisions for a pregnancy? . . . How do we go about obtaining a driver's license? . . . Could we arrange a get-acquainted party for all our refugees? . . . Could someone compile a comprehensive list of all the sponsors with their addresses and phone numbers? . . . Do they really eat with chopsticks? . . . Is there a Buddhist temple in Washington, D.C.? . . . Can I get help with this big dental bill?

Every sponsor was struggling with so many questions . . . but where were the answers?

Each sponsor had given a report and it was my turn. "Mrs. Crist, may we hear from you?"

I stood, pushed back my chair, composed myself, and began to read . . . slowly and deliberately:

No one warned me of the self-control I'd be required to show.
No one warned me of the tricycles in the driveway and the formula in the refrigerator.
No one warned me of the increase in our milk bill.
No one warned me of the bushels of laundry.
No one warned me of the loaves of bread disappearing from my breadbox.
No one warned me that this project would require all my time.
No one warned me of the frequent drop-in of Americanized Vietnamese friends.
No one warned me that I would have to talk so slowly.

No one warned me that my telephone messages would be mislaid and forgotten.
No one warned me that someone would read my morning paper before me.
No one warned me about the high cost of Pampers.
No one warned me of the frequent unscheduled trips to the market.
No one warned me that the rice cooker would boil over every evening.

No one warned me of the gentleness of this lovely family.
No one warned me how quietly they walk, talk, and work.
No one warned me of the kindness each child consistently shows.
No one warned me how earnestly these people try to communicate.
No one warned me of the warm hugs and juicy kisses.
No one warned me of their genuine appreciation.
No one warned me that I'd come to love these children so dearly.
No one warned me of the joy we'd share at mealtime.
No one warned me how much I would learn from them.
No one warned me that the media would find them so newsworthy.
No one warned me that our congregation would care so much.
No one warned me that friends would bring us corn, tomatoes, and beans.

No one warned me that Grandmother Le would do all my mending.
No one warned me of the blessings received as eleven of us pray together.*

When I sat down, there was complete silence in the room. I looked toward the chairlady seated at the head of the table. Tears were streaming down her cheeks!

I learned later that she had eight refugees living in her home. No wonder she was able to identify so closely with me.

---

*This report was later published as a poem titled, "Progress Report." Copyright, Church of the Brethren *Messenger*. Used by permission.

# 17
# I Need Time Alone

My girl friend phoned Saturday afternoon to inquire how things were going. "Oh, Carole," I exclaimed, "I have six beautiful hours all to myself . . . completely alone."

I told her I had taken the family to a picnic at two o'clock and didn't plan to pick them up until eight that evening. The hostess, a beautiful Vietnamese war bride residing here about five years, had invited several refugee families for a cookout.

As soon as I had learned of the plans, I phoned Dale and together we decided I would drive in to meet him and we'd go out for dinner. "Just so we're home by eight to pick them up," I reminded him and he agreed.

I was having a wonderful time by myself . . . doing some of those things I had postponed for so long. I basked in my freedom . . . feeling so good

. . . so free of responsibility . . . when the phone rang. I was surprised to hear Dong's voice and I looked quickly at my watch. It was only 4:30!

"Evamae, can you come for us, please?"

"But, Dong," I remonstrated, "it's only 4:30."

"The children are tired, Evamae, please."

"Okay, Dong, I'll be right there."

As I put the phone down, I burst into tears. All my suppressed negative feelings began to emerge. Couldn't I even have one afternoon to myself? Wasn't I entitled to six hours of peace and quiet? This was my home. They were intruding in my privacy . . . my leisure time. . . . I needed time alone.

However, my rebellion didn't last long. I soon composed myself, powdered my tearstained cheeks, and started off to pick up my family.

I was careful to disguise my true feelings. Dong explained that the children had played so hard and had also overeaten. The hostess had served a native Vietnamese meal.

When we got home, Grandmother Le put Baby John in his crib for a nap while Dong and Anh prepared the other four children for their naps. Before long the house was nice and quiet again.

On the extension I called Dale . . . whispering into the phone that our plans were changed. Would he please come home for dinner instead of taking me out. I went to the kitchen and began peeling tomatoes.

After dinner Dale . . . being very sensitive to my needs . . . suggested that we go for a ride. I had prepared and served dinner . . . so Anh agreed to clear the table and wash the dishes.

Without my knowledge, Dale had picked up two tickets to a drum and bugle corps exhibition scheduled for that night at a nearby athletic field.

We had a wonderful time . . . alone . . . on a balmy summer evening . . . sitting on the bleachers. On the way home we stopped for pineapple sundaes.

A strange car was parked in our driveway when we returned. One of the families from the picnic had stopped in to visit on their way home. Although we couldn't understand a word they were saying . . . we could see they were enjoying a delightful time together.

As I prayed that night . . . I asked to be forgiven of all those negative feelings. God showed me a verse in Ecclesiastes that I shall always treasure, "Fear God and obey his commandments, for this is the entire duty of man. For God will judge us for everything we do, including every hidden thing, good or bad" (12:13, *The Living Bible*).

# 18

# The Fat Man Blesses Me

I could hardly wait for that night! Doug Oldham, the fat man of gospel music, was scheduled to appear in our area for his annual concert. Fond memories of his previous concerts flooded my mind as I dressed for the occasion.

We were backing out our driveway when I thought of it! "Stop, Dale, I must run back into the house." I ran in . . . upstairs . . . into Grandmother Le's room . . . and from the bookshelf took one of my favorite books, *I Don't Live There Anymore* by Doug Oldham. I'm not sure why. . . . I just wanted to have his book with me.

Dale had bought it for me . . . Doug had autographed it for me . . . and I had enjoyed reading it tremendously.

I could sense the excitement of the evening as we entered the lobby. "I hope he doesn't wear that awful cranberry suit tonight," I whispered to

Dale as we walked past Doug's album display and into the auditorium.

"Why, what's wrong with it?" Dale wanted to know.

"He's much too wide to wear red," I answered.

Dale took me to my seat . . . then left to hang up his coat. When he returned he told me I could relax. He said, "I just saw Doug . . . and he's wearing a nice blue outfit."

The lights grew dim . . . dimmer . . . the auditorium was in total darkness. . . . A spotlight suddenly illuminated the round face of that beautiful man in the front row . . . who picked up the microphone and began to sing, "I Love the Thrill That I Feel When I Get Together with God's Wonderful People."

The spotlight followed him to the stage where . . . for the next hour I was captivated by the charisma of this gospel singer . . . his glorious voice singing . . . praising . . . praying . . . weeping . . .

Intermission . . . Dale walked out to the lobby. . . . I casually opened the book I had brought along with me.

I couldn't believe my eyes! There on the first page . . . where Doug had personally autographed it for me so beautifully . . . were red ink scribbles all over! Oh, no, not my precious book! I wanted to scream. . . . I felt like crying.

It all came back to me slowly. . . . Several weeks ago I was helping Grandmother Le with her English lesson in her bedroom. She showed me her notebook where . . . in perfect English and beautiful script . . . with a red felt-tip pen she had written laboriously:

In the morning I get out of bed
In the morning I eat breakfast
In the morning I go to school
In the morning I go to work

She was kneeling on the floor using her bed as a desk. I knelt down beside her and leaned on the bed as I watched her write.

Phuong came over and wanted to be included in the English lesson that morning. I remember Grandmother Le gave her the red pen . . . and inwardly I shuddered. What if she wrote on the painted walls . . . or on the beautiful wallpaper? But I was busy teaching my favorite pupil . . . and promptly forgot about the red pen in the hand of a two-year-old.

I looked again at my book. There . . . beneath Doug's signature he had written, "Romans 8:28." I remembered part of that verse: "All things work together for good to them that love God. . . ."

I wondered . . . did that reference to "all things" include all this scribbling in my precious book . . . and all these hostile feelings I was experiencing?

The second half of the concert was a masterpiece . . . as Doug continued his brilliant performance. The audience sat spellbound . . . mesmerized by the magnificence of this man's voice and testimony.

As I listened to Doug's rendition of "He

Touched Me" . . . I closed my eyes and thought of precious little Phuong. I remembered all those rounds we made together on the tractor . . . she sitting on my lap as I mowed the lawn. . . . Round and round we went . . . me singing loudly over the sound of the motor . . . she trying her best to keep up with the words and the melody.

Suddenly the red scribbling didn't matter anymore. I couldn't wait to get home to hug her and tell her once again how much I loved her.

I hoped she would still be awake!

# 19
# The Mailman Delivers Joy

The mail brought so much love. . . .

My beautiful daughter-in-law, Edith, wrote:

"We are so anxious to hear all about your Vietnamese family and how you and they are adjusting. We got the newspaper clipping on Monday so that gave us an idea of what's happening. We think you are doing a fantastic thing and are sure you will be greatly rewarded.

"We'd like to hear everything. How long do they plan to live with you? Do you cook all their meals? Are they adjusting well to the American way of living? Tell us everything. We know you're busy but please write when possible."

Our dear friends, Bill and Margie, wrote:

"We know God is blessing you and will continue to do so because you are willing to share with others. Your new family is very beautiful. It was great just meeting them and we are looking forward to fellowshiping with them as they become a part of our large Christian family. I know God will bless them. Thank you so much again. God bless you. We dearly love both of you. Much love and prayers."

Arden, the Witness Commission chairman, wrote to the church:

"The congregation and Dong's family are most fortunate that Dale and Evamae were willing to open their home to help in resettling our Vietnamese family. We need to support them with our prayers. Most of us cannot imagine what suddenly having nine new family members in our home would be like."

My precious friend, Milly, wrote me this note:

"Sharing your home with nine strangers is a beautiful thing to do. You'll never know how many people's faith was rekindled, strengthened, and revived by your generosity. God bless you all."

The following note along with a check for twelve dollars came from my friends, Wilma and Don:

"We were in church Sunday and felt richly blessed to get to meet our family—in Christ—from Vietnam. How fortunate we all are to be brothers and sisters in Christ and have such blessed fellowship together! And how very blessed they are to have you, Evamae and Dale. You are extraordinary Christians, indeed, to share your home, prepare meals, do laundry, and the like. I'm sure we who aren't there can't begin to realize how many details arise to be taken care of. Evamae, you are one in a million! I'm sure the joy you receive from doing it is wonderful compensation. God bless you all."

My sister, Colleen, wrote:

"Thanks for the nice clipping about your Vietnamese family. That must be a great experience for you and I'm certain it's very rewarding. It certainly was a nice gesture on the part of your church."

My longtime friend, dear Alta, sent me a check for ten dollars with this note:

"I am sure your joy has increased because you extended your family and love to others. There must be many frustrations and sacrifices but the blessings and joys are more—and His grace is more than sufficient for each task.

"God is good and we praise Him. Your joy in serving gives glory to the Lord. May God continue to use you and Dale as He extends His family through you and your home. Let's keep rejoicing in Him."

Mary Ellen, my cherished friend, wrote:

"We are sorry to have missed seeing you and Dale when we dropped in on Sunday evening. However, we were delighted to meet Mrs. Nguyen and several of the children. We were warmly welcomed and given cool drinks.

"They are lovely! Both she and the children

seemed to radiate happiness and a sense of well-being, all because you have been willing to share your home and yourselves. We know you are giving love and security to this precious family group who have experienced so much suffering and loss.

"Hopefully, we can see you soon. God bless you."

A big box of pencils arrived from our treasured friends, Bill and Ruth from Tennessee, along with this note:

"We thought maybe your lovely Vietnamese children could use these in their schoolwork. We, in Shelbyville, are proud of our pencil industry. Shelbyville became a pencil center because in earlier days, red cedar, of which we have an abundance, was considered the best wood for pencils.

"Bill and I remember so pleasantly our visit in your lovely home. We think of you often and pray God's blessings upon you and Dale."

A prospective sponsor, my friend, Doris, wrote:

"I sincerely commend you and Dale for the great love and dedication you have shown your Vietnamese family. We all anxiously await the opportunity to welcome ours."

And these profound words came in a note from my special friend, Rhoda:

"God is more interested in our availability than He is in our ability."

# 20

# Memories of a Former Homeland

Our evening meal was the high point of each day's activities. I usually served dinner about eight o'clock which is considered late by Pennsylvania Dutch standards but quite common in Vietnam and in the Crist household.

Some of our most memorable conversations took place following our meal when we all relaxed . . . lighted the antique kerosine lamps . . . pushed back our chairs . . . talked and sang. Music plays an important role in our lives . . . and we sang much with our Vietnamese family.

One evening our discussion centered around the United States. Dale and I both shared with them . . . on a very elementary level . . . as much of our nation's history as they could grasp. They seemed to enjoy hearing about the Pilgrims and our religious freedom. We were surprised to discover that Dong, Anh, and Vu were familiar with the history of President Lincoln freeing the slaves.

They seemed to know more about President Kennedy than any other political leader outside their country. Somehow Dale and I ended up singing for them "God Bless America."

Following our duet, Dong suggested that the children sing a song from their country for us. Anh lined the four children up in a row on the patio, straight and tall, and they began to sing. The only word I could understand was "Vietnam."

Dale and I began to applaud . . . for the children were doing an admirable job. The more we applauded . . . the louder they sang. What a wonderful time we all were enjoying!

I happened to glance toward Anh who suddenly seemed to wilt in her chair . . . covering her face with her hands . . . beginning to weep. I tried to comfort her . . . without success. When the children saw their mother crying . . . their singing stopped . . . and the atmosphere speedily shifted from gaity to sadness.

Dong helped her from her chair and together they went indoors. Such a sad ending to a beautiful experience. Dong returned to the patio to tell us that Anh was remembering her country . . . her family . . . and her friends . . . left behind as they had to evacuate without notice.

# 21
# Love in Action

The florist knocked. He handed me a lovely bouquet when I opened the front door. I couldn't imagine why I was getting flowers today . . . no birthday . . . no anniversary . . . no party.

Hurriedly I opened the card and read: "Have a good time. Love from Dong and Anh." I couldn't believe my eyes. I felt so guilty. Why did they spend their money on me? . . . Had my excitement been so obvious? . . . Had I mentioned it too often? . . . Did they know how much this visit would mean to me? . . . Had I talked too much about it?

I was so excited that night as I waited for our youngest son, Johnny, and his wife, Anne, to arrive home! They were living in Virginia . . . attending school . . . he a seminary student . . . she in nursing. They were coming home to meet our new family . . . and spend the weekend with us.

The back door opened and there they were . . . he so handsome . . . tall and dark. She so lovely . . . tall and beautiful. Our Vietnamese family witnessed a real homecoming!

I began the proper introductions. The children and I had rehearsed this whole scene . . . many times . . . and it was going well. "Viet, this is Johnny."

"Good eve-ning, Johnny. How are you?"

"I'm fine, Viet. How are you?"

"Fine, thank you."

I warned Johnny that was the end of the conversation . . . that was all the English we had learned so far. I introduced Johnny and Anne around the circle and the children performed brilliantly . . . all with the same and proper response.

Then we all went to the kitchen for ice cream, cake, chips, cokes, and coffee! As we sat around the table Johnny announced that he had a gift for the family. All looked surprised when he explained that his gift was in the form of a song. Johnny and Anne began to sing. I looked at them in amazement! They were singing in Vietnamese! From the reaction of our family I could tell they understood every word. They were overjoyed!

How did Johnny and Anne know all these words? . . . Where did they learn them? . . . How hard they must have worked to prepare such a wonderful gift for our new family!

Soon the children were singing along. . . . Vu joined in . . . then Dong and Anh. It wasn't long until I began to feel like a foreigner in my own kitchen . . . with eleven of my favorite people singing . . . loudly . . . and with great joy . . . their native Vietnamese songs.

We had always heard that Vietnamese family ties were unusually strong. Tonight they had their first glimpse into an American family with strong ties too.

We all liked what we saw!

As I watched these families blending together . . . I was praising the Lord!

# 22

# Our Necessary Room

Anh loved to listen and I loved to talk. . . . Together we made a great team! We spent so much time together . . . making beds . . . husking corn . . . polishing furniture . . . shelling peas . . . doing laundry . . . but mostly in the kitchen in food preparation.

Anh considered our talks a learning experience . . . a good way to learn conversational English. I encouraged her to express herself . . . even though it often was extremely difficult. We relied heavily on the dictionaries . . . Vietnamese and English translations.

Sometimes she would ask me to tell her the stories again. I knew which were her favorites. I would repeat the exciting stories surrounding the framed mementos on the wall of the downstairs necessary room.

I described the glamorous lives of the first

ladies . . . how it must feel to live in the White House. I told Anh how I prayed for Mrs. Ford every day after she had undergone major surgery. I wrote to the president and his wife expressing my concern. Soon a reply came from the White House . . . thanking me for my letter. I framed it . . . and hung it on the wall of the powder room.

Teddy Kennedy, Jr., was on my prayer list during his ordeal with leg cancer . . . followed by amputation. I wrote to tell him how much I cared. He wrote me a beautiful expression of his gratitude which I framed and hung.

Governor and Mrs. Rockefeller responded with a lovely note when I wrote to Happy about my concern for her undergoing major surgery.

Only the very special momentoes find a place on the wall of our necessary room. There is a picture of Dale and me outside Jerusalem by the empty (praise God) tomb . . . a picture of each of our children . . . and a photo of my favorite niece, Berri.

For Christmas, Vu decoupaged a gorgeous plaque for me . . . a picture of a mother robin feeding her young. Guess where I hung Vu's very special gift to me. . . . You're right . . . on the necessary room wall.

# 23

# Barns Aren't Just for Horses

At breakfast that morning I announced that today we would clean the barn. Our lovely old barn is used primarily for horses, occasionally for parties, and even a hootenanny now and then.

I now had planned a better use of it . . . as a storage place for the household furnishings we were beginning to accumulate for our Vietnamese family.

Anh, Vu, and I . . . along with the children . . . went up to the barn and began to sweep the cement floor. Vu had not swept more than ten minutes when Dong came to the barnyard fence and called him to the telephone. Vu came running back up to tell me that his friend was going to Fort Indiantown Gap. She wanted to know if he would ride along. I sensed his eagerness to go. . . . Many of his friends were still there . . . waiting to be sponsored.

Reluctantly I told him he could go . . . but I was unhappy that he didn't feel any responsibility to stay home and help. After all, I reasoned in my self-pity . . . I was doing this for him . . . and his family.

I didn't realize that morning how much we would need . . . and appreciate . . . this clean storage space the very next day!

I applied the brakes quickly . . . then put my car in reverse. I backed up . . . parked along the road . . . and examined the pile more closely. I saw a bed, a mattress and spring, a rocking chair, an overstuffed chair, two andirons, and a vanity stool along with many plastic bags filled and tied tightly.

I instructed Viet and Quyen to stay in the car as I walked across the lawn and knocked at the door of a nearby house. A lady answered and I introduced myself. I questioned her about the pile out front. She said she had put it all out for trash. A fire in her home recently had caused extensive smoke damage and she was replacing this with new furniture.

I was suddenly embarrassed. . . . Could this really be me . . . standing here . . . begging?

I told the lady that a family of nine Vietnamese was living with us and that we were looking forward to the time when they could move into a home of their own. The furniture she was discarding looked so good to me that I was wondering. . . . "Of course, take what you want . . . but you'd better hurry. The garbage man comes about noon."

"Thank you very much," I said . . . and added

as I turned to go, "God bless you."

I immediately drove out to my husband's business to borrow his station wagon for the moving. I returned home to pick up Dong and Vu. All the while I was praising the Lord that I had passed by that house at exactly the right time.

Dong, Vu, and I loaded the station wagon full . . . but the mattress and spring had to be balanced on the roof. Other motorists eyed us curiously as I drove home cautiously . . . with Vu hanging out the right window . . . Dong hanging out the left window . . . both holding on to the clumsy cargo on top.

We unloaded all the furniture and stored it in the clean dry barn.

# 24
# Blessings from Texas

I was just finishing up the breakfast dishes one morning when Vu walked into the kitchen and asked, "Evamae, may I talk with you?"

I am unaccustomed to this. In our home when someone wants to talk, we just talk . . . there and then . . . but our Vietnamese were so courteous. I answered, "Sure, Vu."

"May I see you on the patio?" he questioned as he walked out of the kitchen. "What now?" I wondered as I put the last remaining utensils away and went out to the patio.

Vu offered me a chair. As soon as we were both comfortable I asked, "What is it, Vu?"

Haltingly . . . but with his very best English . . . he told me he had received a letter from a Vietnamese friend in Texas who told Vu that he and his buddy were driving to Pennsylvania . . . for a visit at Fort Indiantown Gap. He said they would arrive a week from Thursday.

Vu then asked, "May they stay here?"

I hesitated. I really wanted to be kind and cooperative . . . but right now I had all I could handle. . . . I had been working like a slave . . . washing . . . folding . . . ironing . . . cooking . . . cleaning . . . babysitting. . . . I didn't have a free minute to myself. How could Vu possibly ask more of me?

"Vu, I know how much you want to see your friends but I have all I can handle. You must know I am already serving thirty meals every day."

He thought awhile and then said, "Maybe they could eat in a restaurant."

"Besides," I asked, "Where will they sleep?"

I hated myself as soon as I had uttered those words. . . . I thought of our lovely upstairs which still had one unoccupied bedroom . . . and there was an extra twin bed in Vu's room.

Vu answered with a question. "Could they sleep in your garden?"

I knew I was going to cry. . . . I didn't want Vu to see me . . . so I said quickly, "I'll think about it, Vu, and let you know."

With that I got up and left the patio abruptly. I don't remember what Vu did then.

The rest of that day my mind shuttled between self-pity and love. I remembered the Bible verse, "But the Son of man has nowhere to lay his head." I knew that as a Christian I should be willing to serve those extra meals . . . do the extra laundry . . . make the extra beds . . . but I knew I couldn't handle one more thing!

In self-defense I began to rationalize. If those two boys could drive here all the way from Texas . . . think of the expense of the gas and all those meals en route. If they have that kind of money . . . let them take care of themselves.

I really had meant it when I told Vu I would think about it and let him know . . . but I didn't. I never mentioned his friends from Texas . . . and of course . . . he was much too polite to approach the subject again.

The following Thursday evening I was getting dinner. I watched the family out in the backyard playing ball with all the children. Grandmother Le watched from a lawn chair by the fireplace where she sat holding Baby John. They seemed to be having such a good time.

The telephone rang and I answered. A male voice with a heavy Vietnamese accent asked for Vu. I told him Vu had gone to Fort Indiantown Gap for the day and would not return until later that night.

"Mrs. Crist, this is Mike from Texas. Did Vu tell you I am coming to visit you?"

I wanted to scream into the telephone. . . . I wanted to tell this stranger to leave me alone. . . . I wanted him to know I was overworked . . . that I felt imposed upon . . . but instead I heard myself asking him where he was. When he answered, "At Exit 10," I told him to look across the highway for a large white dairy plant surrounded with many white trucks. He told me he could see it from the phone booth.

I instructed him to go over to the dairy . . . ask for Dale Crist . . . and follow him home.

I banged the phone down . . . ran upstairs to my bedroom . . . slammed the door shut . . . and fell to my knees beside the bed. I wanted to pray. . . . I needed help so desperately. But no words came . . . just tears. I don't know how long I knelt there . . . weeping.

I rose from my knees and looked toward my vanity mirror. There it was . . . the first thing I saw each morning when I opened my eyes . . . a white card stuck in the corner of the mirror frame . . . with these words printed on it: "But the Spirit produces . . . Love . . . Peace . . . Joy . . . Goodness . . . Kindness . . . Faithfulness . . . Humility . . . Self-control.

I rinsed my face . . . powdered my nose . . . and returned to the kitchen to finish dinner preparations. As I worked I began to sing a new chorus I had recently learned: "There's a sweet, sweet Spirit in this place. . . . And I know that it's the Spirit of the Lord." I knew then that everything was going to be all right!

Dale, Mike, and his buddy, Lee, arrived shortly. I was so glad to see them. . . . I was happy that they had come. What a miracle the Lord had performed in my life during the last hour!

I served dinner on the patio and pulled up one extra chair. Vu didn't get home in time to eat with us. We had a wonderful time that evening. Mike and Lee had been in the United States about three years. Both were enrolled at the University of Texas and employed in a restaurant. Neither had heard of the whereabouts of his parents or families since the fall of South

Vietnam. They had many questions for Dong who had left Vietnam only five months before. We sat long on the patio that night . . . and talked.

We all waited up for Vu.

We had no problem finding enough beds for our new friends.

As Dale and I lay in bed that night I shared with him my experience of the evening. I witnessed to him how the Lord had changed my attitude instantaneously. Just then the most beautiful sounds began drifting from Vu's bedroom. He was playing my guitar . . . and the trio . . . Vu, Mike, and Lee . . . were singing their native songs. I praised the Lord for allowing me to enjoy this special privilege.

The next morning brought added joy! There were twelve of us for breakfast. The kitchen was crowded . . . so I served breakfast on the patio . . . a beautiful summer morning . . . our home overflowing with love . . . a real reunion for Vu, Dong, and Anh with Mike and Lee. I thanked God for all His goodness to us!

The boys drove to Fort Indiantown Gap. Mike went in search of the girl friend he left behind three years before in Vietnam. Imagine the joy and jubilation that night when they arrived home for dinner to tell us that Mike had found her. . . . What a reunion that must have been. . . . However it didn't last long. . . . She was scheduled to leave the next day for Oklahoma . . . where someone had agreed to sponsor her . . . sight unseen.

But Mike was not discouraged. "Oklahoma is

closer to Texas," he reasoned as he smiled at me.

The next morning . . . following a hearty breakfast . . . the three were off to Washington, D.C. They watched dutifully as I mapped out a route for them to follow. Seeing the White House . . . the Washington Monument . . . and Mr. Kennedy's grave . . . had been their dream. Today it was to become a reality.

We waited until very late to have dinner and when they did not arrive, we ate without them. I was putting the dishes into the dishwasher when they walked into the kitchen. I had prepared plenty of food so it didn't take long to warm it up and serve them.

After the family had gone to bed, the boys and I sat in the den and talked long into the night. I learned so much about their country and its people. Mike told me that Vietnamese family relationships are extremely close and important . . . with strong emphasis on family loyalties and friendships.

He talked about the extended family . . . a phrase I had heard often at the Gap . . . which includes grandparents, uncles, aunts, and cousins. That accounted for the unusually large families at the Gap waiting for sponsors.

Lee told me that education ranks high and illiteracy is practically unknown in Vietnam. As they reminisced, I soon discovered that Vu, Mike, and Lee had been in the same class in high school together back in Vietnam. Only the intellectuals were allowed to remain in schools which were run by the government. Testing was frequent and if scores were less than superior, according to Mike, the boys were sent into the armed forces without question.

Vu had continued his schooling in Vietnam . . . completing two years of law school. . . . Mike and Lee had come to America. As we talked . . . I began to look at Vu differently. Perhaps he should be in college. But his English is so poor.

We discussed religion in their native country. Buddhism is the major religion . . . but the Catholic Church is also very strong.

They talked of the continuing war in their country for almost thirty years . . . of the take-over by the Viet Cong . . . and the collapse of the South Vietnam government in April 1975.

On that grim note we said, "Good-night."

At noon the following day the boys had to leave for Texas to be back when their classes resumed four days later. Before leaving, Mike asked me if he could copy one of my posters. It said: "Don't walk in front of me, I may not follow. . . . Don't walk in back of me, I may not lead. . . . Walk beside me, and just be my friend." I watched him as he wrote. I wish now I had given my poster to him.

We stood in the driveway and said good-bye. Mike handed me a paper bag. I opened it. He had bought me a 1976 calendar in Washington featuring all the points of interest in that great city. I now have it on my desk as a constant reminder of a very special visit from two very special young men . . . and to think . . . I almost missed out on this great blessing.

# 25

# Please Tell the Doctor

Driving home from my second meeting with other sponsors in our county, I wondered how I was going to confront Anh with the birth control session I had just attended. She and I had grown to love and respect each other. We already had some intimate conversations about being a woman, a wife, and a mother, although we always had to rely heavily on our dictionaries.

Anh had given birth to five children. Baby John was only three months old when they arrived in our home.

Dave, a respected physician in our congregation volunteered to provide postnatal care for Anh and Baby John free of charge. I praised the Lord for him as I talked to Anh about her preparation for the first visit to his office. When I gave her all the proper instructions she said, "Please, Evamae, tell the doctor no more babies."

I knew it was not my responsibility to inform the doctor of Anh's wishes. Once again I turned to the Lord for guidance on a very delicate subject.

I was elated when I learned that birth control information was on the agenda.

When I got home I talked to Anh about the sponsor's meeting. I told her we had discussed birth control for our Vietnamese families and that I had information for her and Dong. I handed her a sheet entitled "Methods of Contraception." The front was printed in Vietnamese with the English translation on the reverse side.

Eight methods of contraception were listed: the pill, condom, intrauterine device, diaphragm, cream and jelly, condom and foam, rhythm or safe time, and sterilization or vasectomy.

Beneath each column were the following questions with the appropriate answers given in detail. How does it work? . . . How reliable is it? . . . Are there problems with it? . . . Side effects? . . . Advantages? . . . Prescription needed? . . .

Anh and I talked at length . . . she with many questions . . . I with few answers. . . . We decided her next step would be to share this information with Dong . . . and then talk it over with the doctor on her next visit.

# 26

# Jesus and I Love Them

I loved being with the children . . . and took them with me constantly as I attended to the usual necessary errands involved in running a large household.

The first time Viet and Quyen entered the supermarket with me they were bewildered . . . then astonished . . . at the magic eye opening and closing the huge glass doors. Both continued to go in and out . . . amazed at this impressive invention. Although the children enjoyed watching the magic door operate . . . they did not enjoy shopping inside the market . . . complaining that it was too cold. Vietnam is a tropical country . . . with hot temperatures, dry winters, and wet summers. The children shivered as they helped me shop.

It was a traumatic experience for all the children the first time they rode with me through the automatic car wash. The little girls were actually frightened . . . the boys were in complete awe. After their first exposure to this disturbing experience . . . they seemed to like it. Each time thereafter . . . when we passed the car wash . . . they would point to it . . . and urge me to drive through . . . even when my car was shining clean.

The first week the family came to live with us . . . the boys, Quyen and Viet . . . were invited to attend the day-care center operated at our church. After filling out the necessary forms, I walked into the classroom with the boys and the head teacher.

Although Quyen and Viet were shy and couldn't speak the language, they were readily accepted by the other children. I was amazed how color-blind the pupils were. . . . I saw no evidence of prejudice. Though they were unable to communicate with words, I watched as the children . . . upon the teacher's instruction . . . begin to share their equipment and toys.

As I drove home that first day, I praised the Lord . . . but I also had some questions. How do prejudices form? . . . At what age do children begin to discriminate? . . . When do the minds of children become biased and distorted?

At school each morning Quyen and Viet would kiss me good-bye . . . and continue waving until my car was out of sight. My biggest thrill came at the end of the first week when . . . as I walked to the door of the day-care center . . . a little boy shouted, "Here comes Viet's mother."

I praised the Lord for the pure minds of these

children . . . untainted by all the prejudices of our adult world.

If you enter our den . . . the first thing you'll notice . . . is a large framed poster on the wall which reads: "Caution . . . Human beings here . . . Handle with care." I bought that poster several years ago . . . long before God brought this precious family into our lives. How often I had to stop and remember that advice! Some days I really got uptight. . . .

Although we refer to it as the bathroom scales . . . it is not situated in the bathroom. . . . Rather it is located in the upstairs hallway. I am accustomed to weighing myself every morning at the same time.

Soon after our family came to live with us, I noticed that someone had been tampering with the scales. Each time I looked at the scales I noticed the red mark didn't line up with the zero. I would adjust it . . . but the next time I passed . . . it was out of line again. It was really beginning to bother me.

I never actually saw anyone tampering with the scales . . . but I believed it was one of the youngsters. Every day the same thing . . . every day I would line it up again. Should I mention it? Should I confront the children?

The longer I struggled with it . . . the less important it became. If the children enjoyed moving the dial . . . well, I guess it wasn't that bad after all. I just gave up weighing myself as long as they lived with us. And wouldn't you know . . . it didn't make any difference at all!

I never tired of rocking Baby John. As I held

him I would sing "Rockabye, Baby" and other nursery rhymes. But my favorite lullaby was "Jesus Loves Me." I would sit in the den by the fireplace rocking him . . . singing . . . and thinking . . . maybe some day Baby John will be president! Because he was born on the island of Guam during his mother's escape from Vietnam, he is an American citizen!

It always began with just Baby John and me . . . but invariably it ended up with the other children, particularly the little sisters, appearing out of nowhere. They always wanted to "take turns" with me . . . rocking and singing. As I sang they would hum or sing along. Sometimes as I observed them at play later, I could hear them humming the songs I had sung for them.

What a tremendous responsibility I had for shaping these precious lives. I prayed for them constantly.

Our minister arrived at the appointed time. Following a cup of hot tea and an English muffin with us on the patio, I ushered him . . . along with Dong and Anh . . . into the den where they could talk privately.

The pastor felt it was important to explain the significance of the service they had requested for Baby John.

Earlier I had mentioned to Dong and Anh that the following Sunday a dedication service was planned for the parents of newborn infants. They both seemed genuinely interested. I told them they would be giving Baby John to the Lord. Being Buddhists . . . they were unfamiliar with my frequent talk about the Lord . . . but they did understand references to God.

When the minister had gone, Anh came out on the patio where I was sweeping . . . put her arms around me . . . sobbing as if her heart were breaking. I wondered what the pastor could have said to upset her. Together we went to find Dong for an explanation.

Through her sobs she talked to Dong. He smiled as he told me what Anh said. "Anh thought you meant she would have to give our Baby John away when you said 'Give him to the Lord.' Her tears are those of joy . . . relief she now feels knowing she can keep our son."

How carefully I chose my words following that incident!

## 27

# Grief and Sympathy

My mother phoned to tell me the sad news. . . . Uncle Bob had died that morning. . . . His funeral was scheduled for Tuesday. . . . Could Dale and I please come?

The men had gone to work. . . . The boys were at school. . . . I shared my grief with Anh and Grandmother Le . . . using the dictionaries to translate *death* . . . *funeral* . . . and *grief*. Their moods soon reflected mine . . . sadness and melancholy.

We talked long . . . and in quiet tones Anh told me of the death of her younger brother . . . who lost his life fighting in the Vietnam war . . . the sorrow it had brought to her family. Grandmother Le watched us closely . . . Anh talking to me in English and Vietnamese. . . . Together we hunted the translation. . . . Then the two women would talk in their native tongue and Anh would again share some of her feelings with me.

With pensive eyes Grandmother Le looked at the black patch pinned on front of her mandarin blouse. As she fingered it, she looked wistfully toward me as Anh explained the Vietnamese custom . . . a widow wears a black square for one year following the death of her husband as an indication of her mourning. My heart overflowed with compassion as I looked at dear Grandmother Le . . . a lovely sixty-six year old lady who had lost her husband, her son, her home, and her country in close succession. What a pillar of matriarchal strength! I felt such a deep love and sympathy for her.

That afternoon Anh came to me expressing her sympathy. She held both my hands gently as she looked into my eyes and said, "Evamae, I am very sorry to know about your uncle's death. My family and I express sympathy to you." I was so amazed I could hardly speak. . . . I managed a weak "Thank you, Anh," but wondered how she possibly could verbalize such an inclusive thought.

That night I shared with Dale what Anh had said to me. Both of us marveled at her latest accomplishment.

Performing my usual morning chores the following day, I emptied all the wastebaskets into the outdoor fireplace where I burned the contents. A warm breeze was blowing on a balmy summer morning . . . when suddenly without warning . . . the wind swooped down and lifted several scraps of paper up and floated them across my lawn. I ran as fast as I could . . . finally picking up the last elusive scrap.

I casually glanced at the scraps. There . . . to my surprise . . . was the entire message of sympathy Anh had printed so carefully on the small paper. She copied it from a manual supplied to her by a volunteer agency at Fort Indiantown Gap. She memorized each word perfectly for me. How considerate of Anh!

I explained carefully to Anh our plans to drive to the funeral. It would be a long trip. . . . We would leave before daybreak but would return very late the same night. I went over the menu with her so she could take care of the kitchen duties while I was away. I also made arrangements for the men to be taken to work and the boys to be taken to school.

Dale and I attended the funeral . . . then returned home late that night after the family had gone to bed.

Next morning I was having coffee at the kitchen table when I heard one of the children upstairs. I went to the steps and watched as Viet came rushing down . . . his arms outstretched to me. With great elation he shouted, "Evamae's home . . . Praise the Lord!" I had only been away eighteen hours but he had missed me.

What a thrill! To hear my precious little Viet who knew less than a score of English words . . . say, "Praise the Lord" . . . it suddenly brought a new dimension to my life!

# 28

# Hard Work—Happy Heart

Entering the labor market in the United States was difficult for a Vietnamese military man. The economy was low . . . and unemployment was high. Dong had spent thirteen years in the military and had attained the rank of lieutenant commander in the South Vietnamese Navy.

Jack, a fine Christian young man in our church, accepted the responsibility of helping Dong secure employment. Night after night he came . . . faithfully . . . to our home . . . questioning . . . searching . . . encouraging . . . challenging . . . composing a résumé for Dong.

What an impressive one it was! His language abilities included English and French. He was proficient in algebra, geometry, calculus, chemistry, and physics. He was particularly interested in acquiring a job with administrative responsibilities related to normal business functions.

Betty, our helpful neighbor, served as chauffeur and guide . . . taking Dong with his brilliant résumé . . . from one plant to another . . . day after day . . . throughout our city.

One afternoon as she parked her car in our driveway, I saw Dong jump out quickly and hurry toward me . . . smiling broadly. I knew he had found a job! He told me he would start the next day. He had more good news! Vu also had been hired by the same company. . . . Both would begin together tomorrow. They were to be ready by 5:30 a.m.

We all were overjoyed . . . and felt like celebrating. . . . Instead we concentrated on necessary preparations for Dong's first job. He was required to supply his own toolbox with appropriate tools. That was one major expense we hadn't counted on . . . so Dong decided to borrow Dale's tools until he was able to acquire his own. Plans had to be made regarding transportation to and from work.

As I retired that night I praised the Lord for His continued goodness to this precious family. Now that Dong had found employment, another burden had been lifted . . . and my load seemed lighter.

I didn't fall to sleep easily that night. I was thinking about Dong and Vu and their new jobs in the morning. . . . Would the alarm go off in time? . . . Would they get along all right? . . . Would their fellow employees accept them? . . . Would they be resented? . . . Would they be able to handle the work load after having been unemployed for such a long time?

I got up quietly . . . being careful not to arouse Dale . . . and went downstairs. I wrote a note . . . attached it to one of the two lunch boxes neatly waiting on the kitchen counter . . . letting them know I cared . . . and that I would be praying for them.

I went back upstairs to bed.

# 29

# With This Gift I Thee Thank

About a week later . . . as I was mowing the grass late one warm summer afternoon . . . Anh came running down across the lawn . . . excitedly waving a paper in her hand. I shut off the motor as she approached me. Out of breath . . . but smiling . . . she showed me Dong's first paycheck. She was so pleased . . . over and over she repeated, "Happy day for Dong, happy day for my family."

She asked if I would take care of the children and give them dinner. . . . She and Dong were going out with a friend. I agreed . . . and it was several hours later before I discovered what the secrecy was all about.

That night Dong and Anh gathered all the children around Dale and me in our den . . . then handed us a beautifully wrapped package. Their friend had driven them to an oriental shop in a neighboring city for this very special purchase.

We opened it together . . . and found an exquisite white ceramic elephant . . . handmade in Vietnam. Dong explained that white elephants are rare in Vietnam . . . and when seen . . . tradition holds . . . will be followed by good fortune and prosperity. As they presented it, Dong expressed their gratitude to us for opening our home to them. It was the very first purchase from his very first paycheck.

Another unexpected surprise followed . . . just a week later. When I returned from the hairdresser, Dong and Anh quickly ushered me upstairs into Vu's room where they showed me their most recent purchase.

There on the desk stood a huge rattan swan . . . which they had bought that morning when a friend drove them again to their favorite oriental shop. Dong said they wanted to present this swan to our church as a symbol of his gratitude.

We worked late that night preparing the presentation for the following morning in church. I made several phone calls regarding the service. Anh macramed a lovely yarn hanger. . . . I supplied a photo block. . . . Dale furnished photographs. . . . Betty cut and arranged a lovely fresh flower bouquet from her garden . . . while Dong prepared and memorized a speech. The children were excited as they watched us put it all together.

The next morning Dong walked down the church aisle carrying the swan filled with gorgeous flowers . . . followed by Anh, Phuong, Nguyen, Viet, Quyen, Vu . . . and then Grandmother Le carrying Baby John.

What a touching scene it was as they stood . . . serene and humble on the chancel steps . . . as Dong . . . confident and grateful . . . said:

"We are very happy to be here today to present to all members of the First Church our little gift. The swan represents this church rescuing and holding my family. The fresh flowers represent the new life we are able to begin because of the kindness of you people.

"This is a symbol of our gratitude and we hope that as you see it regularly, you will always remember us with your support and prayers.

"As you know, I have a job and I am happy with the job. We are looking forward to becoming self-sufficient as our children enter school and we become a part of the life of the community and this church.

"Please, Lord, receive our gratitude and give happiness to everybody. Thank you."

# 30

# The Almost Impossible Dream

A new zest and sparkle became evident in Dong from the day he brought home his first paycheck. I began to sense his eagerness to get into a home of his own. Scarcely a day passed that he and I did not discuss the possibility of him renting or possibly buying a house.

When the Witness Commission next met, I shared my concern about a home for Dong and his family with them. With his usual efficiency, Arden appointed my good friend, Joe, as housing chairman.

Joe immediately began following up leads from newspaper ads. I typed a letter to the six leading realtors asking them about available housing in center city close to public transportation, public schools, and Dong's job.

Not one realtor responded. . . . Was it because I included the words "Vietnamese refugees" in my inquiry? Disappointed with my lack of results . . . I turned again to the Lord. I talked to Him . . . simply and honestly . . . and told Him about our needs for a home for Dong and his precious family.

Soon Joe phoned to ask if I could look at some properties with a realtor and him on Saturday. I went to the hairdresser earlier than usual . . . then met Joe at the real estate office.

The three of us inspected several properties without success. By late afternoon I was tired and discouraged when the realtor unexpectedly said, "I've got one more that might be just what you're looking for."

On the way to the property I kept praying that the Lord would direct us to just the right house for Dong's family. My first reaction was very disappointing when the realtor pulled up in front of a house badly in need of upkeep. However, my disappointment was short-lived when we walked inside! It was lovely. . . beautifully furnished . . . with lots of room . . . a good heating system . . . and a very pleasant backyard.

Joe, the realtor, and I discussed a rental agreement and made plans to bring Dong and Anh to inspect the house. All the time I was repeating in my thoughts, "Thank you, Jesus." I was certain He had led us to the right home for the Nguyen family.

During the church service on Sunday morning I had great difficulty keeping my mind on the sermon. It kept wandering off to the property and the plans we had made to see it with Dong and Anh that afternoon. Arden agreed to meet us at the property and Joe rode out with the realtor.

I carefully watched Dong and Anh as they followed the agent through one room after the other, down into the cellar, up to see the bedrooms, and then out into the yard. They did not appear to be as excited as I thought they should be. However, by the time the thorough inspection was over, Dong and Anh were smiling and it seemed certain that this would be their future home. The rental arrangement was acceptable to Dong and as we drove home I was busy describing how I could help them turn that house into a home.

Telephone calls between Joe, Arden, and me filled most of Monday. I was excited . . . and praising the Lord!

Tuesday morning following breakfast, Dong asked if he could speak with me. From the sound of his voice I could sense that something was wrong. I began to feel uncomfortable as we went out in the yard to talk.

He held Anh's hand as we three walked slowly toward the lawn chairs near the creek and sat down.

Dong began, "Anh and I decided we cannot move into that house." I was astounded! When I was able to speak I asked, "Why, Dong, why?"

He hesitated, looked at Anh, and then answered, "Our home must face east."

My mind was racing. . . . Why must their house face east?. . . Was this another Vietnamese custom? . . . Why didn't they tell me that on Sunday? . . . I had already made a verbal commitment with the realtor. . . . What will I tell Joe?

. . . What will Arden think?

I asked both Dong and Anh to wait there on the lawn. I went into the house . . . brought out a paper and pencil . . . rejoined them . . . and explained that I wanted them to write down all the requirements they had for a home.

Dong took the paper and pencil and began to number. After consultation with Anh in their native language, I watched him as he wrote:

1. face east
2. house with three bedrooms
3. center city near primary school
4. garage

The house we had agreed to rent did not face east and did not have a garage.

I phoned Joe at his office. "Joe, you aren't going to believe what I have to tell you," I said.

"Try me," he replied.

So I shared my experience of the morning. He was not nearly as discouraged as I. He agreed to begin our search for a suitable house all over again.

A week later on a hot summer afternoon Joe called to say, "I think I've found it." I agreed to meet him immediately to look at the new house he proposed for Dong's family. Driving in I prayed for the Lord's guidance. I felt so strongly that He had led us to the other house and then Dong turned it down. This time I wanted to be very sure.

I pulled up in front of an attractive red row house in a nice neighborhood with a big shade tree out front. Joe and John, the realtor, were waiting for me on the front porch. If it seemed suitable, we'd recommend the house to Dong and Anh.

A comfortable warm feeling swept over me as I entered the front door. The living room was carpeted and one entire wall was paneled. High wide windows made the living room bright and cheerful. Plenty of room in the dining area . . . then into the kitchen. It needed attention but I wasn't the least discouraged.

We filed upstairs to inspect the bathroom and three bedrooms, then on to the third floor to see the remaining two bedrooms. I could envision what a few coats of paint and some frilly curtains would do for this spacious home.

John took Joe and me to the cellar to see the heating system and the hot water heater. The wiring was in good condition and the plumbing quite adequate.

We walked out into the backyard. The grass needed mowing and the shrubbery needed pruning but the lot had a fence around it. Just perfect for the children, I thought.

As we walked back into the kitchen, John asked, "Well, what do you think, Mrs. Crist?"

"May I just walk through it one more time, John?" I asked.

Joe and John waited on the cool concrete back steps while I took another tour of the house.

I was really struggling and I asked God to guide me. I had been convinced last week that God had led me to the other house yet . . . it was a wrong decision. "Please, God, help me. Let me know if this is the house You have for Dong and Anh."

I took stock. It faced east . . . had five bedrooms . . . school was only one and a half blocks away . . . and a garage was situated at the end of the backyard . . . everything Dong had requested. "Please, Jesus, just give me a sign. This time I have to be sure."

Slowly and thoughtfully I walked through each room downstairs. . . . then up to the second floor . . . through the hall . . . up to the third floor.

I gasped! There it was . . . my answer! Hanging on the wall was an antique plaque . . . I remembered seeing such plaques when I was a little girl. . . . On it was printed "Be of Good Courage." I gently removed it from the crude nail on which it was hanging . . . and examined it closely. It was dusty and fragile . . . brown and oval shaped . . . but still . . . I knew it was my answer!

I thanked and praised the Lord for this sign of affirmation . . . then returned it very carefully to its dusty place on the wall.

I couldn't wait to tell Joe and John that I found my answer! I ran down the steps, through the long hall, down another flight of stairs, through the dining room, through the kitchen . . . out to the cool back porch where they were sitting.

Breathlessly I began . . . but stopped short. They wouldn't understand that God had given me a sign right then and there. Instead I regained my composure and told John that I saw an antique plaque on the third floor . . . since I am an avid collector. . . . He didn't let me finish. . . . John said, "Tell you what, Mrs. Crist. If your friends buy this place, you may have that antique. The owners left it here when they moved out."

I was so certain . . . so confident . . . I had the warmest feeling of inner peace that I was already planning on which wall in our bedroom that plaque would look best.

Next evening I brought Dong and Anh in to the house where we met John and Joe. John carefully explained the heating system to Dong while Joe assured Anh that a few coats of paint would improve the kitchen. We went over the four items with Dong . . . one . . . two . . . three . . . four. Yes, it met all his requirements with additional benefits . . . the green grass . . . the lovely yellow rose bushes . . . the fence around the yard . . . neighbors on either side. I praised the Lord for giving us so much more than we asked.

Dong and Anh agreed they would like to have the house. However, this one must be purchased. . . . No rental arrangement could be made. Because I had that inner confidence . . . I forged ahead.

I called my friend at the bank and arranged a meeting. Ralph, representing the church, and I outlined our needs to the loan officer. I told him about our very special Vietnamese family. We asked the bank to finance the mortgage. Ralph filled out the loan application. Although the price was reasonable, the banker asked for a 20 percent down payment. We knew we would have to ask the congregation to help!

That Sunday following regular services a special meeting was called to consider financing a home for the Nguyen family. Arden presented the plan to the congregation. Would the congregation make the down payment, allowing Dong to assume a fifteen-year mortgage?

A heated discussion followed. Not all our members felt the same way toward Dong as I. Many questions arose from the congregation. Could we be sure that Dong would pay back the money?

I stood to my feet . . . was recognized by the moderator . . . and began. I could not hold back my tears.

"During the past months this family has lived with us in our home, and we have come to love them dearly," I began. "We have been saddened by the stories they have shared with us about their personal lives in Vietnam.

"At one time Dong and Anh lived in North Vietnam. They found it necessary to flee to the South where they lived in Saigon and again had a home of their own," I continued.

"They fled from their home in Saigon fearing a blood bath. They have come to us . . . hoping to build a new life for themselves. I plead with you . . . let's make the down payment, let Dong assume the mortgage payments, and at the end of fifteen years, Dong will own his own home."

I still had not convinced all the members of the congregation that they should supply the needed money . . . but in my mind the message of the plaque kept occurring over and over . . . "Be of Good Courage" . . . I was so certain that God wanted Dong's family in this house that I was willing to fight to the bitter end.

The moderator called for the vote. "All in favor of supplying the down payment for the Dong Nguyen home, please raise your right hand." I was afraid to look around.

"All opposed, same sign. . . . The motion is carried!"

I rushed to my car and raced home . . . eager to tell Dong and Anh the good news. I ran into the den . . . the house was quiet . . . and I began calling out, "Anh, Anh." She came running down from her bedroom on third floor. We met halfway in the upstairs hall. I hugged her tightly and kept repeating, "Anh, you have your house! Anh, you have your house." Overjoyed, Anh began to weep.

The children suddenly appeared out of nowhere. Although they couldn't understand what I was saying . . . they knew that something wonderful was happening with their mother and me. Anh and I laughed . . . then cried and . . . in a sudden outburst . . . the children began to clap. What a glorious celebration took place that Sunday noon in our upstairs hallway! The almost-impossible dream was slowly beginning to become a reality!

Our church people mobilized to help prepare the house for its new owners. Two evenings were designated as work nights. Volunteers turned out by the dozens . . . each bringing paintbrushes or appropriate equipment. The women cleaned and scrubbed . . . the men sanded and painted. Some hauled furniture . . . a baby crib, refrigerator, stove, and mattresses. Others plastered and did repair work.

The house glistened . . . the workers glowed. What precious fellowship. How much they cared! How much they shared!

# 31

# The Dream Comes True

The dream was coming true . . . with each box we carried out of our home and loaded into the station wagon. . . . Where did all these things come from? . . . How did they accumulate so much?

We had carefully planned this day. Dong and Vu would come to the new house following work. . . . The boys would walk to their new home after school.

Our moving day went smoothly. Anh and Grandmother Le knew what each box contained and where each belonged. The little girls ran excitedly from one room to another . . . up and down the stairs . . . examining and exploring their new home from cellar to third floor.

After work Dale took Dong and Vu with him in a truck to pick up the final pieces of furniture . . . from the homes of church members who had generously donated enough to furnish the entire house adequately.

I prepared dinner in my kitchen . . . then took it into the new house. On the dining room table was a lovely bouquet of fresh flowers . . . so beautifully arranged. Anh had cut them from her backyard for this joyous occasion!

What a festive event it was . . . as we sat down together for our first meal in the new home! We held hands around the table as Dale prayed earnestly for our dear friends as they started on the road to self-sufficiency!

Only five months before . . . as Dong held his panic-stricken family together aboard that ship fleeing Saigon harbor . . . as shells and rockets exploded nearby . . . he must have been dreaming of this day . . . when he and his family . . . safe and secure . . . could sit once again around his very own dining room table.

Praise the Lord for all His loving kindness!

It was late when we finished washing dishes and placing all the furniture. Exhausted . . . but very pleased . . . we all kissed "Good-night" . . . and Dale and I drove home . . . alone!

The next morning I opened my eyes. . . . The house seemed strangely quiet. . . . I rolled over and glanced at the clock. . . . It was almost eight. . . . The children would be late for school. . . . I jumped up quickly. . . . Then the realization struck. . . . They are gone. . . . They have moved into their own home. . . . They don't live here anymore!

It was so quiet . . . too quiet!

I looked over at Dale . . . still sleeping. I guess

the labor . . . and excitement . . . of last night had exhausted him too.

I sat up and remembered . . . "This is the day that the Lord has made. . . . Let us rejoice and be glad in it!"

I put on my robe . . . went downstairs . . . brought in the morning paper . . . and plugged in the coffeepot.

I was already thinking of them . . . and missing them.

I went to the phone and began dialing their number.

*Appendix*

# Our Children Comment

KENDRA EVE, our daughter, writes:

I vacillated between pride and warmth for my parents and an uneasy jealousy—rather like the arrival of a new baby into a mature settled family.

Wow! How wonderful for my folks to step from among the masses, risking criticism and skepticism, and offer a home and heart to some uprooted refugees—victims of a corrupt war. Now, that's what the essence of God's love is really all about! What strength! What unselfishness!

On the other hand, I wondered, will there be room for us when we go home to visit? Will Mother and Dad be so preoccupied with their new family and the worthiness of their undertaking that Bob and I will have to take second place—or worse yet—be forgotten altogether in the excitement and novelty?

Even after meeting the Nguyen family, these feelings persisted. I liked—yet resented them—simultaneously.

But when I saw the tenderness in my father's eyes as he watched the children scurry toward him with outstretched arms and heard the gentleness of his voice as he sang "Climb, Climb Up Sunshine Mountain" with them as he had with me nearly twenty-five years ago, a flood of warmth filled me—like the heat that surrounds you as you stand in front of a roaring fireplace.

Perhaps even more moving was my mother—the neatly dressed, socially conscious woman—who entered the scantily furnished home, after the Nguyens had their own house, and without a second thought or glance promptly squatted on the floor to converse with Anh.

These gentle, foreign people had transformed my parents and, to my surprise, had begun to transform me.

JEFFREY DALE, our son, writes:

I was excited about going home but somewhat apprehensive too. I wondered about the changes that may have occurred in my family with the addition of these Vietnamese.

My wife and I tried to prepare ourselves for the change. We wondered if there was enough room for us to stay at home during our visit. Correspondence from home recently had been practically nonexistent so we were aware of the total commitment my parents gave to this new family.

Frustration began to build within us along with jealousy. These people must be very special for my parents to devote so much time to them.

I can't honestly say I was anxiously waiting to meet them after driving 2,000 miles. Edith and I were eager to get home and be with our families again. But I did want to satisfy my curiosity. I wanted to see if a foreign family could adapt itself to our frantic, industrious society.

After meeting Dong, Anh and their children, I began to understand why Dad and Mother put so much time and energy into helping them. To open up our beautiful home to a family of nine took so much love and unselfishness. I admire my parents tremendously.

It was hard to accept at first, but later I was gratified to know that my bedroom and bathroom were being used by persons who were so much in need. They must have felt very much out of place and alone.

I found the children lovable and eager to explore. Dong and Anh were warm and friendly and adjusted well to their new surroundings.

Our time spent with the family was short. But during that time they shared a few of the terrible tragedies they had encountered. I felt quite ashamed of my previous attitude of jealousy.

I sensed in them a feeling of peacefulness. They seemed so free. Finally after months of running they could again lead normal lives.

JOHNNY DALE, our son, writes:
Dear Mother and Dad,

Well, praise the Lord! I applaud you! The task

you've undertaken during the last few months causes my faith in you to soar!

Frankly, I never thought you'd do it. When they came, I never thought you'd last. You've proven yourself to be true to your word, to the Lord, and to us!

Anne and I pray daily that we might be completely yielded to the Holy Spirit so that He might live out the life of Christ in us. Coming home provided a good opportunity for Him to perfect us.

The first time we came home after the Vietnamese family had arrived, I didn't realize how attached I was to "things." It was an effort for me to accept those Vietnamese children running around our house as if it was theirs.

I didn't want Vu sleeping in my bed. Even though I hadn't slept there since high school days, it was still my room, I reasoned.

Their presence in our home caused me to look into some dark areas of my life that the Holy Spirit has been wanting to expose.

I do want to share with you a concern of mine about our Vietnamese family. I am concerned about their spiritual welfare. I believe strongly that Christians should be concerned about the destiny of those who have no relationship with Christ.

When I talked with you earlier about that, Mother, your response to me was, "Well, we don't want to push them."

Amen, you're right. A decision to follow Christ cannot be an argument; no one has ever been forced into heaven. But something more has to be done. They trust you. You two have their confidence. Don't you think more could happen?

I just found out from one of the fellows here in seminary that there is a church in Lancaster for Vietnamese. Do you think that you could get Dong and Anh in touch with someone from there? Mother and Dad, I'd just love to see that whole family get saved.

You've made me so aware of our responsibility to entertain angels unaware. My heart goes out to the family. I need these frequent reminders to tell me to allow God's compassion to be given freedom.

You two have indeed sparked faith in me. I can't help but believe that your story should have eternal consequences.

This sounds more like a theological treatise than a letter but I just thought I'd like to tell you how I feel.

Love,
*Johnny*

A picturesque and pastoral scene aptly describes Evamae Barton Crist's birthplace at Pinto, Maryland. Under the secure guidance of devoted parents as the youngest of three children she was well trained for the leadership roles she would later assume in her social action and community affairs.

A conscientious objector to the war effort in alternative service married the farmer's daughter and whisked her off to Pennsylvania where they reared three children. Their one daughter and two sons are all happily married and living in the West.

Teaching Sunday school brought a refreshing impetus to her life as other duties required more of her time.

A busy homemaker and wife, Evamae lives with her husband, Dale, in the countryside of Hallam, Pennsylvania, where she continues to pursue her varied interests.

You may contact the author at:

Evamae Barton Crist
Route 24 (Hallam)
York, Pennsylvania 17406

Telephone: (717) 755-5118